My Mother's Garden

By
Julius C. Manrique, Ed.D.

AuthorHouse™
1663 Liberty Drive, Suite 200
Bloomington, IN 47403
www.authorhouse.com
Phone: 1-800-839-8640

AuthorHouse™ UK Ltd.
500 Avebury Boulevard
Central Milton Keynes, MK9 2BE
www.authorhouse.co.uk
Phone: 08001974150

First published by 1st Books Library 6/22/2006

ISBN: 0-7596-3808-X (sc)

Printed in the United States of America
Bloomington, Indiana

This book is printed on acid-free paper.

Cover by Milda Laukkanen

First printing in 1999

This book is dedicated to my mother, and the many fine and intelligent women teachers that I had as a student—thank you.

All characters and events in this book are true. The author experienced meeting these individuals and encountered these events during his formative years and professional career. Some events describe direct contact with people and others were shared with them either during meetings or after interviews. In some situations fictional names were used to more clearly explain certain incidents.

Contents

Preface

After spending more than forty years in education as a teacher and an administrator at all levels from K-6 to the community college and being asked by many to put some of my personal and educational experiences in writing, I reluctantly decided to do that upon my retirement. All of my educational experiences have taken place in Stanislaus County, mainly in Oakdale Elementary School, Oakdale High School, Modesto City Schools and Modesto Junior College (part of the Yosemite Community College District). The characters are real, but names have been changed to protect their identity and the innocent. The personal experiences are true and actually happened, but the items expressed are my personal experiences and feelings.

The book starts with a reflection of my past as I grew up and was educated and acculturated mostly by American women teachers. One of fifteen migrant children, I was reared/raised by Serapio and Mary Manrique in Oakdale, California. I wish to thank all my brothers Primo, Vincent, Lawrence (deceased), Arthur (deceased), Joe, Raymond (deceased), Edward (deceased), Richard and Tony, and sisters Dolores (deceased), Linda (deceased), Jenny (deceased), Alice, and Madeline (deceased) for their inspiration, guidance and influence during my formative years.

During the nineties, we have read of the success of many minorities, i.e. Mexican American, African American, Asian American, Vietnamese, Hmong, etc., but when I grew up on the East Side of town, we were just called "those Mexicans." All of us who grew up on the East Side of the tracks were poor, so we didn't notice any differences or how the wealthy lived. We accepted what little we had, without question!

This is another story of how one lifts oneself up by sheer determination without any financial help from anyone and under the most adverse social and economic conditions. This story proves the statement of President Thomas Jefferson,—"once you educate the masses you will have set them free." Education freed me from poverty and set me free to help, and influence many who came into contact with me.

A special thanks to the women in my life—my mother who instilled all the values, ethics, and determination in my life; Miss Ulrich (1st grade teacher) who showed kindness and interest in a very shy boy; Miss. Karoline Ardis (4th grade teacher) who influenced how I taught through sheer poise and respect for students, classroom management and neatness; Miss Ditto (8th grade teacher) who taught me the love of our country and instilled in my mind the democratic form of government; Mrs. Kellas (Flying A Station Owner) who, through her kindness, gave me a piece of candy every time I brought my report card to her that led to perfect attendance all through school, including college and forty years of employment (missed three days); Miss Mary Phillips (Junior College Spanish teacher) who helped me improve my reading and writing of the Spanish language; Dr. Lillian Gray (Professor of Education at San Jose State University) who displayed teaching techniques I used throughout my career; my wife, who provided the rudder and the foundation to our marriage; and to my daughters, who helped me understand how to be a parent and a father.

A special thanks to Linda (Borello) Prouty who typed up the first draft in 1978; Thuy Ngoc Pham who computerized the second draft (in 1997) and added much to the completion of this document; the many proof readers such as John A. Garcia, instructor at Modesto Junior College; Jean Marie Miscisin, a writer and publisher in her own right; and the many others who have prodded and inspired me to finish this journey through life.

1. The Garden

This particular spring morning I was outside admiring my mother's beautiful roses, blue iris located in front and the sweet peas that were planted along the south side of our house located on 157 North Fifth Avenue in this quiet little town of Oakdale, California. All of a sudden I heard sounds of cattle to the north and I could see dust as they made their way towards our home that was located on the edge of this little town. We lived on the east side of the tracks that had few electric lights; no sidewalks, curbs, nor gutters; and the streets were mostly compact dirt. If you could picture how the poorest lived, this part of Oakdale would be one step above that. Most of the homes in our area were just slapped together to provide shelter and to keep the rain out of the houses. We would have to tar paper the roof of our house almost every other year because rain water would drop in somehow – we had pots and pans all over the place during the rainy seasons. Only the poor whites, Filipinos and Mexicans lived on what was called the East Side of town, so the large land and cattle barons had no fear that we would complain of the mess the cattle made and the dust they created as they passed by. They used Fifth Avenue because it was the shortest route from their pasture land north of the town, over the bridge that crossed the Stanislaus River, down this street, past the cemetery south of town, and into the stock yards near the Santa Fe railroad where the animals were loaded into cars and shipped to other parts of the state.

I ran into the house and shouted to my mother, "Mom, Mom, the cows are coming." I didn't know the difference between a cow and cattle until much later. I was only about five years old and hadn't entered school yet. My mother got her broom and then we both went out and stood on our open porch that faced the street. The cattle were moving by smoothly making dust and dropping their dung all over the place when all of a sudden several steers must have seen these beautiful flowers and charged right for them. They were eating them and tearing some of them from their roots. My mother got her broom and started to hit them to chase them away, but they continued to eat all her sweet peas and irises. I went out and started to scream at them when a cowboy rode his horse right over some of the flowers and shouted at both of us to leave the animals alone. He then reared his horse to frighten us and shouted, "You Mexicans ought to go back where you came from." "You black Mexicans don't belong here in the first place and you should get out of here." He reared his horse and stared down at me and I saw that mean look in his eyes. I could never forget that moment and would remember it for the rest of my life.

They drove their cattle down the street leaving a mess in our front yard. My mother was in tears as she viewed what was left of her garden. I asked my mother what that man meant by saying, "Go back where you came from?" I was born in this house on 157 North Fifth Avenue – where would I go? Also, I asked, "Why did he call us black Mexicans?" I was very light skinned and none of my brothers or sisters were black. She said, "Never mind what he said— go to school and someday be better than those kind of people."

As I helped my mother clean up the mess that the cattle had made, I said to myself, "Someday I will meet that man again and I will show him and his boss that we are not dumb, ignorant, and poor Mexicans." I would be educated and discover this home of ours was property of our ancestors, land that was stolen by the United States by outright fraud and deception in 1848. I guess that ignorant cowboy didn't know that or else he wouldn't have said those things to us. That incident had a tremendous impact on me and remained in my mind a long time. Seven years later my father, with the help of my sister Dolores, purchased a small piece of property from that same land baron. We planted grapes, walnuts, beans, strawberries, and tomatoes and made a decent living doing it. My father packed a box of tomatoes and asked me to take it to that same cowboy who damaged my mother's garden. He didn't recognize me, but I will never forget the look on his face when I said to him, "These are yours and you might want to give some of them to your boss"—the large land baron of Oakdale. We also gave him strawberries and black eyed beans – each time my dad would ask me to deliver them

2

to rub their nose into it. The cowboy never recognized me, but what pleasure I got making the delivery.

Later after my undecided teenage years, I struggled my way through university and received a teaching credential. Guess what? I then taught children of that cowboy and the land baron of Oakdale. At that point they both recognized who I was and that I was from that "Mexican family" on the East Side of town. I apparently gained a lot of attention at that school because I went on to join the Lions Club and became a Scoutmaster and leader in the district. After accomplishing most of my goals that that cowboy instilled in my mind that spring morning by destroying my Mother's garden, I decided to move on to greener pastures. This book relates some of the events that occurred during my journey though life.

2. The Family

More and more, I found it hard to believe that it was possible to succeed in this city, county or country! How could a poor, "Mexican," from a family of fifteen migrant children and parents, who had been migrant workers all their lives, possibly achieve anything in life? My father Serapio Manrique was a fine looking man, stood erect and was very proud of his heritage, his former country and home. He never talked too much about his family in Mexico, but I did have the opportunity to meet his brother and two sisters when, as a student at Mexico City College, I visited Leon, Guanajuato in 1957. The Lord blessed us all with certain characteristics, and, if we are fortunate to have the opportunity to develop them, then we can, in turn, contribute something to society and mankind. I feel my father had a gift for helping people. He understood poverty and loneliness. He tried in his own way to alleviate some of those things in helping those who worked for him, but he never fully understood how to become successful in this complex American society, partly because of the deep distrust and prejudice towards Mexicans by many in mainstream United States. Of all the minorities, the Mexicans are really the one hated and treated the worst, more so than the blacks in many of the states in the Western United States. He had seventh grade education in Mexico but mastered the Holy Bible, mathematics and history. He read both English and Spanish newspapers and books. As he lived his life with a large family, I got the feeling that all that he hoped for (a large ranch, financial security, and successful children) would not be achieved in his lifetime.

Frequently he would talk to me about his home in Leon, Guanajuato, Mexico, and how as a boy he worked on his dad's "rancho." To most Mexicans that would mean a large acreage, but for my father it was a small piece of property—ten to twenty acres. He never fully described where it was located nor did I really question him about the property. When one is young and you hear things like a "ranch" you are really impressed, especially if it comes from your father. Growing up in America, a "ranch" would be considered hundreds and hundreds of acres and that impression was left with me when my father spoke of his home. This illusion was shattered when I visited Mexico later in my life. I feel that today many Mexican families are told of the good times that they had in the old country by their parents, but much of it is fabricated and not too accurate. I knew that my father did not deliberately lie to me, but he shaded the truth a little in order to relieve the pain that he was suffering for not having something to pass on to his family. All he could pass on at this time was a beautiful illusion that things were great in Mexico. This is fairly typical in the older generation of Mexicans that came in the late 1800s and early 1900s—they wanted to impress their families just a little, even though it was not necessarily true. I discovered later that, in Mexico, less than five percent of the people own over ninety-five percent of the good farming land. This also applied to the wealth of the country although, under the various administrations, the middle class grew larger. His love for working outdoors and the desire to please his father was very important to him.

He never fully described him but he did mention that he was a tall, light skinned and nice looking man. My grandfather (my father's father) apparently was born in Spain, but this has not been verified.

It is certain that the name came from Spain similar to most Latin American names. I realized this through my study of Spanish literature where I discovered Jorge Manrique, the very famous Spanish poet. Also while reading Mexican history, I found out that there was a navigator sailing with explorer Cabrillo. Later, when I traveled to Madrid and Toledo. I encountered my family name on several churches and buildings. We make no claim to being related to the former or the latter, but this information is introduced to indicate that the name is Spanish. When I was in Spain, I did not have time to research my grandparents on my father's side too much, because I didn't feel it was that important at the time. At this point of my life, I realized one's environment, heredity, ethnicity and cultural background—all have much to do with your success in life. The church one belongs to, the social clubs that one joins, the political party you advocate and the people you stroke all contribute to your success in the American society. My father was baptized a Catholic, and he was forced to go to church because in Mexico that was the thing everyone did. This had a tremendous impact on our family because he did not force any of us to go to church. My mother was the main stay behind making us go to church. She had a blind faith in religion, whereas my father was turned off religion once he left Mexico.

He never mentioned his mother (my grandmother on my father's side) or ever described her to me; therefore, I know very little about her other than she was a very religious person and made him go to church on a regular basis. When I visited Leon, Mexico in 1957, I met both of my father's sisters (my aunts). They were fair skinned, a little on the heavy side and short. I gathered from that that my grandmother must have been a combination of both of them.

In Mexico when my father was growing up there were very few avenues for success—either you became a priest or you joined the army. There was little opportunity for higher education unless one was wealthy or extremely gifted. The latter, the church made priests out of them, and the former, their parents made sure that they had a good education in order to control their wealth. The two mentioned avenues were the only opportunities offered for young men in Mexico and this pretty well holds true for many even today in the poor classes. The only other life for a country peasant was to head north and find some work in the United States. Things haven't changed very much. There was no opportunity for Mexican women other that to go into the Church or get married and have a large family.

My father left Mexico at the age of sixteen because he did not want to become a priest or be forced to join the army. The government was enlisting young men so he fled north because he did not want any part of the corrupt army. Somehow, with little funds, food and few friends, he made it to the State of Colorado late in the 1890's. He spent several years in that state working on the farms during the summers and living in hovels during the winters. He met someone in 1900, made his way to the Central Valley of California,

6

and settled in Oakdale, California, (approximately one hundred miles southeast of San Francisco). He landed his first job working on a dairy, and he stayed there over a year. He moved from there to working for the Sierra Railroad Company laying rails because the pay was a little better and the hours were more regular. He worked very hard at that job, and he became very familiar with the Oakdale/ Stockton area. At that time, as a young widower with two children (Primo and Dolores) he met my mother, Mary Hopkins Martinez.

My mother was born in Newman, California into a family of five. She was the eldest and attended only three years of school. Her father (my grandfather) was an Englishman who was a seaman during his youth. He was a tall man with many talents. He could play several instruments (i.e. guitar, accordion, violin and piano). I was five years old when he died, and I never fully remembered him, but my older brothers and sisters knew him very well. We have several pictures of him and the family in their musical group, playing and entertaining people in the area. He met my grandmother (a native Californian) in San Jose, married and moved to the Newman area where my mother was born. They later moved to the San Jose area. I did not get to know either of her parents, but she would tell us many delightful stories about her parents. My grandfather was talented in music and taught all the members of his family how to play an instrument—accordion, guitar, violin or piano. They played at various neighborhood dances and parties from the time my mother could remember. My mother learned how to play both the piano and guitar. She also became a very good dancer. She danced beautifully right up to the time she had her stroke in 1977. The uselessness of her left arm and leg and her immobility probably led to her final stroke on February 25, 1978. She could not dance or play an instrument anymore and felt very useless. She was unable to do many of the things she did when she was healthy.

My mother met my father in Stockton, California, and she married at the age of eighteen and remained married for thirty-four years until the death of my father in December, 1952. She never remarried, so, in reality, she remained faithful to my father for a total of sixty years. During their marriage, they had fifteen children with three deaths leaving a total of twelve living children, nine males and three females. Each member of the family had many good characteristics and attributes from both parents. These range from artistic, musical, athletic, intellectual talents and the ability to work hard at a given task. The work ethic was instilled in our family very early in life. My father labored in the fields and so did all the family from the time they could walk. We followed the fruit season in the Sacramento-San Joaquin and Santa Clara Valleys—but always returned to our home in the little town of Oakdale where we had a small two-bedroom home located on the east side of the tracks at the edge of the town on Fifth Avenue. The street was located at the edge of town and would be called a "barrio" these days.

The economic necessities of life kept us laboring in the fields and prevented us from enjoying all the benefits of the American educational system. This certainly affected my older brothers and sisters because they left school early in the spring and returned late in the fall after school was well under way. When my older brothers and sisters did go to school, they were always two to three months late in the fall and they were taken out of school two to three months early in the spring in order to work in the fields. There were no laws making education compulsory, so parents did pretty well what they wanted. My dad needed them to earn money in order to live. So he just took them out of school when the crops were ready. Consequently, they got seriously behind in school, and the older ones dropped out. In the early thirties much prejudice existed towards Mexicans (it hasn't changed much in the 90's) and my older brothers and sisters experienced much prejudice. They were ostracized by the principal of one school and were told to go to a segregated school that housed all Orientals. At that time, the Orientals were also feeling the pains of being a minority. Apparently on this one occasion, my father confronted the principal and told him, in so many words, that all children are supposed to be treated equally and that his children were going to school where all the "white" children were. I couldn't imagine my father challenging the white establishment, but he did succeed in having my brothers and sisters placed in the school where there were plenty of white faces. Regardless of this effort, the other children made it very difficult for them. They would be teased because of the clothes they wore and the kind of food they brought for lunch. This caused them to eat their lunch by themselves and automatically segregate themselves. The principal got his way after all—by using the students to do his work.

Unfortunately, with the exception of Dolores, they didn't complete high school. At that time only the wealthy and those who had much guidance and encouragement from teachers finished the twelfth grade. It was considered quite an accomplishment to finish high school during the 1930s, but for the lower class and minorities a job and work were more important than going to school. It is very important in the Mexican family that the oldest son has a good attitude, characteristics and education because he sets the pattern for all those that follow. My older brothers wanted very much to go to school, but economics and severe social problems permeated our society when they were growing up. The only avenue for them was to find a job, hang on to it, and get married and have a family. All of my brothers obtained good jobs working in factories or industrial plants and made a good living. My brother attempted to buy a small farm after being released from the army. Lawrence and Primo applied for a loan through the Cannery loan system, but when the loan officer asked them their nationality, they were told that they didn't make loans to "Mexicans." This was quite a shock to my brothers, but they had no recourse. In those days, the office of civil rights was not around to help minorities as it is in the 90s, so they swallowed their pride and never tried again.

The questions should be asked – how did I not only complete high school but go on to receive a Doctorate of Education with such a poor economic and social environment and background? Well, that is a long story, which should be told in order to help many other young minorities who might be in the same economic and social situation that I was. I owe much to my mother, and the words she repeated over and over again, "Go to school and be somebody," rang through my mind time and time again as I encountered difficulties and problems throughout my educational career. I should indicate here that all of my younger brothers and sister completed high school. As I reviewed the different personalities in our large family, it was interesting to note each individual had special characteristics. Some were artistic, musical, eloquent, athletic, knowledgeable and clever. All possessed a strong work ethic instilled by my parents. This may have had an adverse affect because we were taught to work but not really to use our talents. An entrepreneurial sense was never encouraged or instilled in us, although some did go into business later in their lives. Our lives may have been different if my father had taken a farming business chance during World War II. As it was explained to me, he did have the opportunity during that period but didn't want the responsibility of running a large farm nor taking advantage of a situation while the Japanese farmers were held in the "internment camps." My father was approached by several Japanese farmers, who owned large farms in the Delta area, to take over their land while the War lasted. They knew that their land was going to be confiscated, but they had much faith in my father because he had the experience of a labor contractor helping them with crops each year. My father felt that it was too much of a responsibility and too political to get involved especially with the attitude of the whites towards the Mexicans during that period. He later told me that he was sorry that he didn't help the Japanese farmers because their farms were stolen and many were never paid for their property. Only years later did the Congress of the United States make some reparations for the property and businesses that these people lost during World War II.

Education was a little different for me and my young brothers and sister. The main reason why we finished was that my mother overruled my father about school and work and insisted that the younger ones not be taken out of school during the fruit seasons. Instead, we worked each night after school until dark and on Saturdays and Sundays. We fully understood that we needed to work, and we worked hard for our father. We respected him, and we knew we had to work in order to survive. We picked cherries, apricots, peaches, grapes, tomatoes, strawberries, and helped harvest beans, walnuts and almonds during the summer months, and then we pruned these same fruit trees and vines in the winter. The time spent in school was a vacation from work, and we learned to appreciate that very much. This type of labor gave us an appreciation of indoor jobs that were to come later in our lives, but this type of labor does have a toll on a person's body as we found out later in life. Several of us had laminectomies in order to correct ruptured discs in our backs. Others have had major surgery due to heavy exertion and strain on the bodies early in life. Yet, we were still more fortunate that our older brothers and sisters not only because we went to school but we learned from their experiences, especially in the area of family responsibilities. When they were married, the family came first, and they got the first job available. They didn't have all the social services that were available during the sixties and the seventies. This family responsibility had an effect on me early in my life. It displayed to me that I could not "have my cake and eat it too." I had to sacrifice the immediate gratification in order to accomplish something in my life. There was no married life in my immediate future, especially while I was working my way through college.

3. Elementary School

What made me complete all the education that I now possess? It started very early in life. I remember my mother taking me to the first grade on the opening day of school. She was working in the local cannery at the time and left me on the playground of the Oakdale East Side grammar school (presently the site of a Ramada Inn). This school looked like a huge factory to a little, shy five-year-old. I saw all the other children playing games and running around laughing and just having a good time. I was rather bewildered and confused as to what to do on this huge open, strange, desolate field which was called a playground. When the school bell rang, all the students ran to the shed where they all lined up to enter their respective classrooms. I did not follow the rest of the boys and girls, but I did walk slowly to the entrance of the shed that housed bicycles and other school paraphernalia. At the entrance stood an elderly lady waving to me to come in; I waved back and I turned around and went home feeling that this wasn't the place for me. Strange that that same feeling came back to me on many occasions during my struggle in life at various political and social events. I made my way across the main street and went to a friend of my mother's across the street from our home. She was a kind and gentle woman just like my mother, and I felt very secure in her presence (something like today's baby sitter). I had a little snack of pan dulce and milk and stayed there until noon. When my mother came home from the cannery for lunch, she was very surprised to see me home from school so early, and she took me in her arms and said, "Remember, school is very important, and, in order to be someone, you have to go to school." Then after lunch, she took me by the hand and walked me back to school. We met the woman or principal who seemed very old and mean, and then we went to the classroom to meet my first grade teacher. She was very friendly and introduced me to the class. I quickly felt a part of the class, and I made up my mind then that I would abide by my mother's wishes. The year moved by very quickly, and school ended. The harvest season began for us.

My school days were similar to other poor children in the area--we just attended without much counseling, guidance, and hope because we would graduate into the migrant labor force regardless of our educational background. Our expectations were not too high, nor did the teachers feel we would amount to much. My older brother and sister had graduated, and they were still working in the fields. Filipino friends of the family had gone beyond high school, and they were still pruning trees and cutting asparagus in the Delta area. What difference would an education make for me? The years went by, and I found myself in the eighth grade. I received an award because I had five years of perfect attendance. That award really impressed me, and with subsequent positions in life, my attendance has almost been perfect. With the exception of three days when I had two wisdom teeth removed, my work record has been almost perfect. This leads me to believe that students should be rewarded or praised for many things besides sports and/or good grades. This same characteristic has been passed down to my two children--you can count the number of days they have missed school on your right hand.

There were few teachers that impressed me with kindness, attentiveness, concern, and neatness along the way through my education. My first, fourth, and eighth-grade teachers were the real examples for me. I have never forgotten them, and I have, throughout my life, tried to emulate them in one way or another. Many things remain fixed in the minds of youth as they move from grade level to grade level. Some teachers are good, and others are there because of their secure position and could not find another occupation. Some really should not be there because many do not care for students or children in the first place. The teaching profession may not agree with me on the latter statement, but as I moved from the elementary level to the secondary level and finally into administration at all levels, I found some really good teachers and some very poor ones. As a principal, I did make many attempts to get rid of the poor ones, and I succeeded in a few cases. That doesn't make you very popular, and I know it hurt my career later because I was thought of as being too aggressive and hard nosed--a little rough around the edges, as I was told by a Superintendent.

There were several times during my school days that would have changed my attitude about people and the educational system. That "kind" first-grade teacher, the "mean" old elementary school principal, and that "awful," grouchy third-grade teacher, the "neat," "immaculate" and "kind" fourth-grade teacher, and a very "wise," "intuitive" and "considerate" eighth-grade teacher, all left a very deep impression upon my schooling. Let me explain these levels in more detail because they had an impact on why I chose the teaching profession and why I remained in that field for over forty years.

The first-grade teacher met me and my mother with a friendly, sincere and warm smile. She accepted my mother and me into the classroom and displayed this with the touch of her hands (heaven forbid touching students today), facial expression, and the sincere words that were spoken. She showed an interest in a bewildered, shy boy and displayed that feeling to my poorly dressed and uneducated mother. The principal may have been as kind as the first-grade teacher, but this was not transmitted during our exchange. I guess she was the disciplinarian of the school and had that reputation among the students. Her face was as impassive as a stone wall. The third-grade teacher had the same characteristics, but she never smiled. She was firm, and all the students were afraid of her. What a shame to have that aura at such an early period of children's education. I remember being pushed into a little scuffle with one of my best friends by some bullies. We got into a little wrestling match, and this particular teacher saw it happen. She never gave me the opportunity to explain, and she physically punished me in front of the class to make an example for other students of which not to do. I have never forgotten that time, place, and event. I learned "what not to do" from that person. In today's terminology, she was over the hill and should not have been teaching children. My third-grade year was a long and fearful one because of this teacher.

Thank God for the fourth grade. It was entirely different. The fourth-grade teacher was a lovely person and was extremely immaculate. She was neatly and beautifully dressed, and it appeared she always wore black. Her hair was always in a bun style and not one hair out of place throughout the day. She was really a model for me to emulate later in life. In my opinion, it is very important for young children to have excellent models during their formative years and that means the early years of school for all children, regardless of their backgrounds. She was respected by all the students.

What a contrast it is today (1990s) with open, unstructured, sloppy classroom situations that exist in some of our schools. Many teachers dress as poorly as the students do because they want to make the students feel comfortable and be their friends. They should hear what the students say and how they criticize these teachers---from kindergarten through college. I have heard much of this criticism as a student, teacher, principal and dean and as a parent of two daughters. Teachers are models and they have to dress and act accordingly. If they don't want to accept that responsibility, they should leave the profession. During the sixties and seventies our educational profession admitted many inadequately prepared individuals, and it certainly has had its toll upon the educational system.

I remembered going into the fifth-grade. After about four weeks of school, I was called out of the room for a very important counseling session. I remembered standing out in the hall with the principal, fourth and fifth grade teachers. They were talking away, and they kept looking down at me. It appeared that it was a very important meeting, and they were really discussing me and my fate at that school. I knew that I did nothing wrong because my mother was not there nor did I see the paddle that we all heard about. It was a rather important conference because they were deciding my future, but it didn't appear to be very scientific or educational. There I was, this little four-foot, 65 lb., boy looking up at these tall, giant women. I was very small, shy, young, and bright, and they were discussing my future at that school. The fifth-grade teacher wanted to put me back into the fourth grade because I was too small and shy for the fifth grade. She felt that I needed more time to mature. The fourth-grade teacher said no because I was too bright to repeat the fourth grade. I was nine years old and in the fifth grade. I missed the second grade and didn't realize that had happened until this scientific and educationally sounding committee meeting taking place in the hallway. After a truly outstanding committee meeting of these three individuals, it was finally left up to me to decide. All of a sudden all three looked down at me, and the principal asked me the educationally sound question, "Do you feel you can do the fifth grade work?" I had been in class for about four weeks (I guess I was on probation and didn't realize it), and I passed everything that was given to me without taking a book home or any help from my brothers or poorly educated parents (my mother had three years of education and my father had seven)--how was I to answer the question? Can you imagine the situation I was in? I wondered what I did to deserve this astounding question? I surely didn't want to repeat the fourth grade, so I said, "I want to stay in the fifth." They all agreed, and the fourth grade teacher said, "I know you will do well in school, Julius--just keep up the good work."

What a lesson in human nature, friendship, tenderness, kindness and encouragement that was displayed by a person who remained part of me all of my life. The following school years were not too eventful until I entered the eighth grade. It was there I met another very kind women who displayed many of the characteristics shown by my fourth grade teacher. I made above-average grades in all my classes without any problems or without taking any books home. There was no use in that because we didn't have the space at home to study. I made top grades in social studies because this wonderful and interesting teacher knew and loved students. All the students liked her and enjoyed the class. It was in this class that I began to understand our form of government because we all had to pass the Constitution test before we graduated. I had memorized the various articles and amendments so well that I could repeat them in my sleep. I not only got one of the highest grades in the class, but I got a lot more. I wanted to be a teacher just like my eighth-grade teacher and teach social studies just like she did. Little did I know that I would be teaching social studies years later in that same room. It was at the eighth-grade graduation that I received the honor of attending fives consecutive years of school without missing one day. I did so because I liked to be in school and I wanted to do everything I could do to please my mother and my fourth-grade teacher. I guess those formative years set the pattern for my educational career. During my entire college work, I never missed a class or lecture. Sickness or adversities never kept me away from a lecture or from completing a classroom assignment. Why? Because I valued education too much to let it be wasted by cutting classes like many students.

4. Boy Scouts

The eighth grade was important to me for another reason. This year affected me profoundly. It was in the spring of my eighth grade year that I overheard two of my classmates talking about the "Boy Scouts." They were going to have a meeting at the high school gymnasium at 7 p.m. I went home and asked my mother if I could join and she asked, "What are the Boy Scouts?" Finally, after some more questions and some reasonable answers, she said I could go as long as it didn't cost anything because we didn't have any money.

So after dinner, this little twelve-year-old made his way across the tracks, through the West Side of town. After walking over a mile, I made it to the high school gymnasium. I opened the door and there they were-- a mob of boys just having a great time. I was so nervous and uncomfortable because again I felt I didn't belong here. I closed the door and with tears in my eyes started to walk home. I made my way to the tennis courts east of the high school, sat down, and began playing with the nets. I remembered what my fourth grade teacher said, "You can do well in school, Julius, just keep it up." I turned around and walked back to the gym, opened the door, and walked across the floor where I met the scoutmaster. He was in a brown khaki uniform, and he said with a smile, "What's your name, and do you want to become a Boy Scout?" I said yes, but I did not know what the scouts were all about. He then sat down with me and went over some material in the scout handbook. He said it cost fifty cents to join, and my eyes dropped suddenly. I remembered we didn't have any money to spare at home. He must have realized and sensed this because he handed me the scout manual and said, "This is yours." I kept that book for over fifty-two years and then returned it to his son who was quite a collector of scouting items. Little did the scoutmaster know that he was to have a tremendous impact on my life. I never did pay the fifty-cent registration fee nor did I pay for the handbook, although as an adult I donated much of my time and money to this program that gave me the opportunity to see how the other half lived. I made my way through the ranks: tenderfoot, second class, first class, Star, Life and finally Eagle. It took many years to obtain the latter, but it was worth it.

Each of these ranks gave me the opportunity to meet other boys and adults. I remembered the map drawing for one of the first class requirements very well. The engineer of the Oakdale Irrigation District was the person in charge of the requirement. I must have drawn that map of Froggy Lake that was north of Oakdale a half dozen times until it was accepted by the assistant scoutmaster. I learned how to draw and write neatly after that experience. I vividly remembered the birdstudy merit badge also. We could not pass the requirements in the valley because one could not find many of the species here. The scoutmaster knew that I could not afford the cost of summer camp at Camp Bob McBride, but he knew that I wanted to go in the worst way. Little did I know that the local bank president sponsored me and paid my way to summer camp. I somehow convinced my parents to let me spend a week away from working so I could take advantage of this offer. From the day I joined the Scouts my mother was saving pennies from my dad's pay checks so that she could buy me some scout equipment, such as a sleeping bag, cooking kit and a pack so I could be like the other boys. When they both agreed to let me go and then gave me this equipment, my heart just raced with joy! How could my poor, poor parents afford to give me this chance of a lifetime?

I guess they realized how hard I worked (as my brothers did also) in the fields after school and on weekends so that I deserved it. I feel they had much more intuition than we gave them credit for. My parents must have known that this son had a little different attitude about school and other things such as the scouts. In their poor humble manner they were going to give me a chance to break through the barriers that have held so many Mexican-Americans down to the lowest levels of economic, social life, and possible achievements.

My dad knew I could read his Spanish newspaper "La Opinion" at the early age of ten. He knew that I could use math as well as he could and that I understood how many square feet there was in a acre and how many plants it would take to plant one acre. He used to give me the problem, and I would work it out for him. We planted twenty-eight acres of grapes that way in the early forties. A phrase he repeated to me over and over again in Spanish was--"Educacion es mejor que oro, porque puedes perder su oro pero nunca pierdes su educacion." My mother would send me to the store with a verbal list of groceries to buy, and I would buy each item and return with the exact change. They knew how dependable I was and that I would make up all the work I missed while I was at camp. I would pick and cut more than enough fruit during the summer to more than pay for the lost time at camp. Yes, they knew a lot more about me than I thought. May I say here that when my younger brothers reached the scout age, they were also given the same opportunity, but their interest in Scouting was not as great as mine. They enjoyed fishing, hunting, camping, and the love of the outdoors in a different manner than I.

My interest in the Scouting movement as a boy was deeply instilled by the joyous experiences that I had in camping, hiking, and working outdoors. These experiences along with meeting successful adults were filed away in the back of my mind to be used when I had the opportunity to be useful in the Scouting movement as an adult. Many of the requirements that were difficult to achieve were accomplished because it took tenacity and discipline to finish them. This helped me later in my life when I was to experience many disappointments, physical problems and emotional letdowns. I was able to convince my parents to let me go a second summer, and it was as enriching as the first one. The experiences confronted by a poor boy from the East Side of the tracks in a middle class environment were too numerous to enumerate. I hope to bring them out during the course of this book, but one that stands out is the ability to accomplish a task.

Disciplining the mind to achieve without the help of others is very important. This attribute was instilled in me, and throughout the rest of my life when I participated in scouting, education, politics and social events, I really didn't have to depend upon anyone with the exception of my wife. This developed a kind of lonely personality because I had to sacrifice some things for later gratification. In my scout troop I was the only Mexican from the East Side of town. At that time I never gave it much thought, but in reality, the Boy Scouts of America was a program sponsored by the middle and upper middle class and the Mormon Church, which, in my opinion, had a lot of influence in the direction that it went. Many of the goals and objectives of scouting were decided by very few while the masses of lay people did the work with the boys in the leadership areas such as scoutmasters, den mothers, etc.

I have nothing but affection and loyalty towards this organization regardless of some people who are in it for personal and egotistical reasons. In reality, there are some adults who are just big boys who have never grown up. They continue to collect and trade patches and adorn themselves with medals, patches and awards. They sometimes forget the real reason why these organizations exist. I will come back to this part of my life later in the book.

5. High School

My graduation from the eighth grade was a usual one. I received a few awards, but my best friend received the Legion award. This award was given to the most popular person in the class who was supposed to have good grades and the most helpful student in the eighth grade. The criteria set up for selecting students for this award were really unattainable, but it would be terrible for a school district if a student wasn't selected each year. The bottom line was really a popularity contest for the students by the students, teachers, and the administration. I remembered vividly being on a selection committee later as a teacher, and I voted not to give one because I felt there was no one who met the criteria. I was joined by a few other teachers, but the administration overruled us. Public relations was the reason given. I realized at this time awards are usually given for social and political reasons, and those who receive them usually know the right people. I dwelt on this subject a little because when I taught at this same school one of the older staff members told me that I was nominated by her but because I was so shy and unassuming I was not selected. I wonder if race and social class had anything to do with it? An Anglo-American had always been the recipient of these awards, and during my tenure, no other nationality ever got the award. This established in my mind and convinced me that it is not what you know in life, but it is whom you know that really counts. In this case I had to agree, but in many other situations the awards are a farce. This friend of mine did go on through high school and continued to do well there and also in college. He was a "poor white boy" and lived several blocks from me. We had an expression, which we used now and then to depict our living conditions. Today our children have "wall-to-wall carpet in almost every room," but we were lucky to have "wall-to-wall cardboard on the floors."

My home was on 157 North Fifth Avenue in Oakdale, California. It had two large bedrooms, a large kitchen area, a small living room, a porch and a bathroom with no bath or shower. One bedroom wall was built on huge hinges so it could swing open away from the kitchen to serve as one large room for parties that my parents gave almost every weekend. They would invite friends over, and they would dance way into the late hours while we watched or fell asleep on the floor. After World War II was over and my older brothers came back, they had seen how the others lived, so they started to convert this old house into something livable. They installed a water heater, gas heating, and more electric lights, a larger bathroom with a shower (hot and cold water) and some carpet in some of the rooms. We were really in "hog's heaven" with these new items in the house.

How this large family got by, I don't know, but we did. It was a miracle. I do remember sleeping with three others in one bed for a long period of time, and many times we slept out on the porch during the summer months. Before all the amenities, we had a wood burning stove, and it seemed that we were always cutting wood for it. My father stuffed the walls with newspapers in the winter months in order to keep the cold air out of some of the rooms. I guess he was ahead of his time because he was recycling material long before it was fashionable. Sometimes during a heavy rain the roof would leak, and out came the pots and pans to catch the water that came through.

It was years later that the house was fixed up so we could enjoy some of the amenities that our neighbors had been enjoying for years. My mother enjoyed her new refrigerator and almost new gas stove mentioned earlier. We actually had a light switch near the door put in for our living room while all the others in the house had the chain type, which hung down, in the middle of the room. Yes, this was home until I was thirty-one years old.

The home that we presently own is a far cry from the one I had as a youth. Although, people who have these wonderful material things and who are in debt still don't seem happy to me. There is always that need to keep up with the neighbors and all that competition that goes along with it. However, when I grew up everyone was poor around our neighborhood, not many people had these luxuries. We accepted the fact that we were poor and got by without the anger that exists today in the nineties.

I just turned thirteen as I entered high school in the fall of 1945. The next four years were really wasted because I didn't know what I wanted nor did I receive much advice or counseling. It wasn't heard of then at Oakdale High. Most of us just floated along through high school, but those who knew where they were going to college got help from staff and were placed into college-prep classes. I remember a teacher telling me to take mechanics and plastics because I could use those skills to get a job. I did what I was told and took mechanics and plastics. Well, the former did help me understand the automobile later in life, but I never did figure out how the latter helped.

All I wanted to do was to be popular by playing sports like my older brother. Well, I realized very soon that I was too small for football, but being stubborn I went out anyway. I got kicked around hard a few times, and I knew this wasn't for me. I gave that up very quickly. This had to be a game for boys who had guts and a tremendous determination to play this sport. It is a shame that our schools have become training grounds for the professional teams, but that is the way it is in this society. This applies to all types of sports. Our whole sense of values and priorities has been turned around, and the students lose their sense of direction when there is such a heavy emphasis placed upon sports. The academics are lost in the shuffle, and the attitude of helping your fellow person in the community is completely lost in our present educational community. The attitude developed in some of today's high school sports program is to get as much as you can and "the hell with everyone else." This attitude has accelerated in many parts of our society and has had its effect through increased suicides, rapes, murders, personal bankruptcies, robberies, divorces, and the lack of standards for the general population. Where will it end?

It was very unrealistic for me to play football in the ninth grade because I was very small, light and uncoordinated. I did manage to play a little basketball and run a little track during my four years in high school. I was fairly successful in basketball but all the other sports were a disaster. I didn't realize why my basketball experience was so poor until later in school I found out my eyesight was poor and I needed glasses. I compensated somehow with this sport and managed to make the traveling team. Boy, did I learn about coaches and their personalities.

When I was a freshman, I also learned about prejudice. My brother, who was four years older than I, was a great player. He had all the attributes of a potential great athlete, but he had one problem. He was vocal, a Mexican, and he was darker than most Mexicans at that time of his life. Somehow he managed not to play on the "A" team because of a very prejudiced coach who had a filthy mouth. He was later asked to leave the district, but he left a very deep impression in my mind of how mean some people can be. I mentioned this about my brother because many members of my family had excellent attributes and talents, but somehow no one really took the time to help and encourage them to achieve. I know it is up to individuals to look out for themselves and raise themselves up by their boot straps, but if we were given a little more encouragement from those who have succeeded, the trip up the ladder could have been easier. We were all destined to the fields of hard labor. I was a towel boy as a freshman and traveled with the team. This particular coach would always single out my brother when we traveled through a colored section of a valley town, and he would yell to my brother, "Hey, Manrique, we're going through the colored section of town--do you have any relatives here?" and then laugh. Oh, how that hurt! My brother would fire some statements back. These were verbal blasts that left a deep impression on me. Why would an adult in such an influential position be so mean? Little did I know I was to suffer similar prejudicial remarks later in my life. I have to believe that the darker your skin is, the more prejudice and discrimination a person suffers. An expression which I picked up during the early fifties that has remained a part of me was, "If you are white, you are all right; if you are brown, you can stick around; but if you are black, you better stand back." I was a very light-skinned Mexican probably inherited through my father who was almost pale and my grandfather Hopkins who was an Englishman. Throughout my life, I would never be considered by most people as a Mexican. With our name, people would first say I was French or Portuguese. It was almost laughable to see how ignorant and lacking any foreign language most people had when they tried to pronounce, let alone, write my last name. After I told them, my father came from Mexico, their mouths would drop open with disbelief.

However, this worked to my disadvantage during the years of affirmative action, because many employers would hire the obvious "black" and "dark skinned Mexican" or Chicano in order to meet their quotas. My name does qualify in order for the "white" employers to hire under the affirmative action guidelines. I found out my education and qualifications for leadership position didn't help me --it came down to quotas, the right people on the selection committee and who you knew, before you were awarded a top salaried position. This was only the beginning. You see, I knew I was poor but so were many others in my small circle of friends. I saw how the wealthy boys and girls in my class, with pretty and expensive clothes, got the best grades, class offices, and the attention from the teachers. I remembered wearing the same pair of pants all year long with hand-me-down shirts and a sweater---that was the extent of my wardrobe. My shoes had to last a year and could not be resoled for the lack of money. We placed cardboard in the inner soles when the soles wore out, but that didn't help in the wet and cold winter months. I sometimes wondered how we survived through that period of our lives.

There were very few teachers who impressed me at the high school level and none like my first, fourth and eighth grade teachers. I often wondered why some teachers were in the classrooms? Some were unable to keep any form of discipline, let alone impart some knowledge. I recall my sophomore year in an English class--we had over a dozen teachers for that class. How could we learn under those conditions? Others were poor managers and were unable to manage a class for more that fifteen minutes and that was used to take roll. My biology teacher was a fine person--soft spoken, neat and well organized. I did enjoy that class and his teaching techniques; a math teacher who gave me a little encouragement; a short obese physical education coach who had a heart of gold and always helped the under dog. He was a pleasure to work hard for. I really learned from him how to motivate students so they could enjoy school and work hard at the same time. I also learned from another physical education coach, who was a frustrated professional reject, how not to treat people. From the time I could remember meeting this man until today, he had an extremely poor way of teaching. He never smiled and he always considered himself perfect--probably because he felt so inferior unless he was in command of a classroom of students. He told students at the beginning of each semester that he never made a mistake and if you found an error on your paper don't bother to ask for a correction. In my opinion, he was a disaster (only there because he couldn't find another job) and a poor example of a teacher and coach. He only catered to the ones who were talented and the relatives of the previous "star athletes" His prejudices were displayed in a very subtle manner and I learned how not to be or act from this man.

6. College

I graduated from high school without any real skills, honors, significance, direction, goals in life. The night I graduated there were many tears in my eyes--that June of 1949. I don't remember a thing other than hearing the well to do boys and girls saying they were planning to go to Cal, (University of California at Berkeley), C.O.P. (now the University of the Pacific), and M.J.C.. (Modesto Junior College). These were all strange and unfamiliar words to this seventeen-year-old senior. Not once could I remember, throughout the four years of high school, any teacher mentioning these to me or even referring to them in my presence. Oh, how I wished I could have gone to college at that time, but Modesto Junior College, which was only sixteen miles from my home, was an impossible dream for me. Although it was such a short distance from our home, it felt like five hundred miles away, and the cost was something else.

Little did I know that the only cost was your books at the Junior colleges. U.C. and the College of the Pacific were in a strange part of the State as far as I was concerned, so I just forgot about them, but M.J.C. remained in the back of my mind--some day. I graduated from high school into the migrant labor force, and my father took us to work in the fields the next day. My four years in high school did not contribute anything to my future at that point in my life.

We started to harvest apricots, peaches, and later grapes for a large Italian farmer whom my father had worked for all during the Depression years. I got my fieldwork "in-service" training with this man. He was a good man and always had a cigar in his mouth. He helped our family get through some pretty rough years and most of us worked for him year after year. As a matter of fact, my oldest brother has worked for him all his life, which amounts to more that sixty years (In 1998 he was still working for his son since the Italian farmer and his wife had passed away.) My oldest brother was a sharp individual, but as was typical in our family, he married young in life, settled down, and raised a family. He never once moved or looked back at what he should have done with his life.

The Italian farmer gave me the responsibility of running a small crew of Mexican workers from Mexico. I could only say a few words in Spanish at that time, but I learn how to communicate fast. My father did not teach us the language because he felt we should learn English first since we would be living here all of our lives. He and my mother spoke Spanish around the house but not with us. This formulated some of my opinions on bilingual education, which were to crop up during my professional career.

It was during my tenure in these fruit fields that I met a Filipino who changed the course of my life. We were pruning peach trees during the dead of winter in 1949 – 1950 making 30 cents a tree and pruning about ten trees a day. It was one wet, cold, frosty, and foggy day when he suggested that we should try to go to M.J.C. and better ourselves. He said we had a brain and graduated from high school, so let's give it a try. I talked it over with my mother, and she was elated that one of her sons was even considering going to college. Then I talked it over with my father, and his first comment was that it costs money to go to college and that my back was stronger than my mind. I realized what he was saying since none of his sons or daughters ever mentioned college to him. However, he was a person who realized that education was the only way out of poverty and the life he had given his family was not the best.

We agreed that I would work after school, weekends and during vacations in order to help support the family because he was getting older and couldn't work as hard as before. I worked hard that year and saved about one hundred dollars. I purchased a few clothes, and I was ready to enter a new way of life. A life of the middle and upper class. After the first semester, I was ready to drop out. My grades were atrocious to me--two B's and all the rest were C's. I really had to struggle even to get those grades. But that wasn't really too bad for someone who went four years through high school without ever taking a book home. My study skills and critical processing skills were terrible, and I started to look for a full time job because I just knew that I couldn't make it though college with those grades.

My Filipino friend got married at the end of the semester and that shocked me into reality. If I quit school, certainly I would get married and that would be the end of college life and my dreams for me. Somehow, through hours and hours of studying the following semester, I made better grades and then gained some self-confidence. I also met a blind man in my economics class. He always got A's in every class that I had with him. I approached him one day while he was having a cup of coffee and asked him how he did it. He called his reader over and we went through the process that they went through. I said to myself that if he could do it with his handicap, certainly I could do it with all my faculties.

I tried what they did and I saw improvements immediately. I had to learn how to study and think before I could make better grades. I applied all my energy and all the time I could spare for studying, and my future suddenly looked a little brighter. My next obstacle was finance. How I would have welcomed some of that Federal financial aid to help me through college. The students, in the late sixties and after, really had it made with the help of some enlightened and farsighted congressmen. Can you imagine being paid to go to school? I guess I was too independent (or ignorant) to ask anyone for help; on the other hand, there wasn't anyone to give me a helping hand that I knew. There were very few brown faces at Modesto Junior College when I attended. As a matter of fact, there were fewer than a half dozen in 1950 – 1952. The standards were very high, and those who couldn't meet them either dropped out or they were not encouraged to stay enrolled by the counselors, advisors and teachers. The staff reflected the same ethnic ratio as that of the students. There were no brown or black faces on the staff when I went to Modesto Junior College. It didn't make any difference to me because that was the way it always was in my educational background; and, as far as I was concerned, at that time, it wasn't going to change for a long while. The county schools' office and all the schools in the county never employed any native Mexican-Americans to teach their students during that period. A few individuals from Latin America were hired in some schools; but, to my knowledge, I was the first native born Stanislaus County, Mexican-American to be hired in Oakdale in 1956. Stanislaus County was a typical valley county that had individuals who tolerated Mexicans, but encouraged the use of their backs to labor in the fields for cheap wages. Mexican-Americans in the schools and the county were tolerated and they were very docile; consequently, there was never a demand to have teachers of Mexican descent. There was no such thing as affirmative action in the San Joaquin valley at that time, and the Mexicans knew their places.

I met a wonderful Spanish teacher at the college who gave me a lot of encouragement. (Later I found out she was of Portuguese ancestry.) Each time she returned the tests and mine was really marked up with red ink, she would write words of praise and encouragement on them. It really hurt to see those red marks on my papers, but each time they became fewer and fewer with more and more praises written on them. Boy, did I learn a good teaching technique from that person!

Another teacher who comes to mind was a good friend, person and teacher. He was also the basketball coach who taught hygiene along with many other duties. I was sailing along with an "A" in his class until the final. We had to turn in a term paper, and it had to be typed. I didn't have a typewriter, and I discussed it with him. He said I could have an extension and that I could take it to his office later. Somehow I got it typed and took it over to his office in the gymnasium. He wasn't in, but there were two basketball players in his office at the time. I asked if the coach would be back, and they said yes. I placed the term paper on his desk and asked the players to call it to his attention when he returned. I thought everything was fine until I received my grade at the end of the semester. I received an incomplete in hygiene. I was shocked and made an appointment to see the coach. All of my experiences that I had in high school with those biased and prejudiced coaches began to emerge in my mind. This man never once gave any indication of being prejudiced, biased, haughty or arrogant. As a matter of fact, he seemed to be the complete opposite—well-liked, confident, friendly, courteous and humble. I sat down to talk to him, eyeball to eyeball, and immediately he put me at ease with a smile and he said, "OK, Manrique, how did I goof!" This overwhelmed me because here was a college instructor admitting a possible mistake. I felt terrible to have filled my mind with anger because somehow something went wrong that neither of us had caused. I told him that I had an incomplete grade and that I had turned in the paper. I had two witnesses that could prove it. He called in the two players and they told him that the paper was placed on his desk and then he excused them. He asked what grade I thought I should get and I replied an "A" because all of my other grades were the same during the semester. He agreed and changed the incomplete to an A. Little did I realize that our paths would cross again, and I would be working with him during my adult life. I learned fair play, honesty, humility from this man and that there were some good coaches/teachers around the college.

The following semester moved by quickly, and my scholastic standing rose slowly but surely. I could never make the honor roll, but I got passing grades. That would have to wait until I worked on my Doctorate and received several honors at the University of the Pacific. I learned a lot from students, teachers, and administrators. I guess my biggest lesson at this level of education was that I learned what not to do and how not to treat students and people. My convictions were solidified, and I became stronger internally. I became more and more independent because I found that there was a lot of cheating, stealing, and conniving going on by some students, and there was much prejudice, bigotry and hypocrisy displayed by teachers at all levels of education. This made me more determined than ever to become a teacher so I could do the opposite of what I had seen during my years in school.

I didn't participate in any extra curricular activities in college because I needed to support myself and my family. This was my biggest burden while I was going to school. I was always wondering how the family was or if they had enough to eat or how were we going to pay the next month's utility bills. I either had to work or study all the time in order to stay even and above water. If I could encourage students to do anything in college besides studying, it would be to participate in some activities while they were there. This is so important in order to find out what is available on campus because these events are a microcosm of the social and political events that take place in real life. They also can lead to a profession or community activity that one can participate in after securing an occupation. This makes you a more useful citizen. This would have helped my personality a little, but this was not to be because my time was very limited. I would go to work as soon as school was out. By the way, I rode the school bus thirty-two miles a day, along with many others because very few of us could afford a car, let alone the cost of keeping one running.

I had little counseling during my entire educational career because my impression of counselors and their services was very low. This impression instilled in my mind a bias against this service in the educational system. If you had good teaching and a dedicated staff, there would be little need for so many counselors in a school system. I took the catalog and prepared my own two-and four-year program without any help from anyone. A person who can read well, they may not need this expensive and sometimes useless service.

June rolled around and I graduated from Modesto Junior College with an AA degree in 1952. The ceremony took place between the North and South Hall in the Greek amphitheater (the present site of the Morris Memorial Administration Building). There was a huge crowd, and my parents and relatives came to see their only son to graduate from college. I guess I brought a rather large cheering section, for when my name was called, a great roar went up, and I was rather embarrassed as I walked across the stage for my diploma. After the ceremony, my mother and dad gave me a big embrace, and tears were just streaming down their faces. They had a son who graduated from college! I introduced my parents to my excellent Spanish teacher for she really was the one who gave me the encouragement to do better and succeed here at M.J.C. My dad asked me what I was going to be? I said a teacher, and he looked at me a little puzzled because he wanted a doctor in the family. I did receive a Doctorate (Ed.D.) but not an M.D. degree. Then he said to me, "Un maestro es mejor que un doctor, porque vas a influenciar mas gente que los doctores." I didn't fully understand what that meant until many years later when students came back to me and told me how I was the one to have helped them. Oh, I could not describe the happiness in my parents' eyes and their faces. It was a miracle that had happened to our family. I was the only child out of fifteen to have graduated from a school beyond high school. This has happened in many Mexican-American families throughout the United States, however, not many families in Stanislaus County. Education was not really encouraged by the parents of migrants. Why should they encourage their children to enter a world of bigotry and hypocrisy? Would it not be better for their children to work the land for a few months of the year and then return to their native soil in Mexico? Who would employ a brown face in an office, school, bank, social welfare department or in a leadership position overseeing whites! No! There would be little encouragement from parents who worked in the fields.

During the summer, I sent enrollment forms to UCLA and was accepted. I wanted to go there, but I had no idea of the cost involved. I was determined to save, scrape and work my way through the next two years of school. As I reflected about my first two years beyond high school, I realized how important the development of the junior college (later community college) system was. This gave opportunity to thousands of individuals like myself to live at home for two years and then transfer to a four-year institution as a junior in college. Somehow my plans were changed by another Filipino friend who lived a block from my home in Oakdale. He had just gotten out of the Army and decided to attend San Jose State University, just eighty five miles away. He would come home on weekends, which suited me very well. I could easily help my parents on weekends. I quickly sent my transcripts and enrollment forms and was promptly accepted. I enrolled at San Jose State in the fall of 1952.

These were difficult times because of the Korean War, and many students were volunteering or being drafted. I took my physical, and I was ready to go into the service when I found out I was rejected because of a curvature of the spine—a bad back. This was really a psychological blow to me, for I really wanted to fight for my country like many Mexican-Americans. I knew then and there that heavy work was not in my future. I studied harder and harder to get the best grades possible. This was my first time away from home and in an entirely different environment. I stayed in a boarding house for one month, and I just couldn't stand the messiness, late hours, yelling, drinking, smoking and just plain wasting of time that went on there. I found one of a number of small and very inexpensive rooms in a home that an elderly partially blind man rented to four boys. This was what I needed-a quiet room with kitchen facilities. It worked out very well, and it was located on 33 Devine Street. I paid $10.00 a month for rent, so you could imagine where I was living and the condition of the house. "Bernie" was the owner, and he was partially blind but wise as a fox. He was retired and extremely intelligent—we enjoyed talking at times for many hours. With a roommate's help I got a gardening job after classes, but I would go home on weekends to help the family. I worked my schedule so that I could have all my classes three days a week and then I could work the other two days.

7. University

The first quarter at San Jose State College just flew by, and I did fairly well. There was a break before the next quarter, and I went home for Christmas. My father was quite ill and had a cough that wouldn't go away. We took him to the doctor, and he gave him a prescription, but it didn't seem to help too much. We didn't have any extra money or any type of medical insurance to put him in the hospital, so we did the best we could. I remembered the last time I saw him living was about six o'clock in the morning when I left to return to San Jose State to register for the next quarter. I looked at him in bed and said, "Dad I'm going now!" He looked at me and, said "Si se puede cumplir su escuela" (Yes, you can complete your schooling). Here was a man who worked very hard all of his life with very little to show for his years of labor. His dream was to own a farm, have some security and live a comfortable life. None of this would come true for him!

He had worked in dairies, railroads, and picked fruit as a migrant eking out a living the only way he knew and very proud not to ask anyone for help or have his family go on welfare. His family work ethics had been instilled in him which meant taking care of his family one way or the other but not asking anyone for help. He passed this work ethic down to his family. For example, the eldest son worked over sixty years for the same farmer; the eldest daughter worked for a hospital for more than thirty-five years; the next son worked for a paint company thirty-nine years (retired at the age of seventy-five); another son worked in the field of education forty years; another son worked in a metal shop for more that thirty years; another son worked for a can company for thirty-five years; and the youngest son worked for another can company for more than twenty-five years and took an early retirement. My dad did instill, in the immediate family, the work ethic and an independence that would be hard to beat by the younger generation.

He managed to save a few dollars and purchased twenty-seven acres of desolate, run down land east of Oakdale. This was land owned by that same large rancher who moved his cattle past our house in town when I was younger. We did not know that at the time. They laughed at my father when he purchased it for one hundred dollars an acre. We later learned why. Other farmers had tried to make this land grow something, but they had failed and had gone broke. The land then returned to the original owner. My father was determined to succeed where others had failed. He purchased a young, beautiful, brown horse (named Danny) and a four-foot spring tooth harrow, and with the backs of four young sons, ages seven through thirteen, set out to prove these people all wrong. That poor Mexican would show these people how to work that soil and make it produce. With the help of that Italian farmer mentioned earlier in the book, the soil was broken up with a caterpillar tractor and a six-foot disc in November of 1945. Then, my father broke it down further with the four foot harrow. During the month of December, we set out stakes in a very old-fashioned manner, eight by ten. Then, my dad recruited many unemployed friends to help plant the grape vines we had pruned from other vineyards. They were planted with tender loving care, and little did we realize that four years later they would be bearing grapes. During the next spring, the vines started to bloom, and our vineyard was on its way.

My father worked the land like a tenant farmer in the deep south—a horse, harrow, and four young boys doing all the labor. He planted tomatoes between the grapes, and they flourished so well that first year that he almost paid off the mortgage. The next winter we planted black walnuts every forty feet. The following spring they were in bloom. We didn't know anything about walnuts, but my younger brother and I grafted the trees to regular walnuts. We were quite successful, and if you saw the trees now, you wouldn't know the difference between our trees and the ones purchased from a nursery. We planted tomatoes the following year, but they were not too successful because of the weather conditions. We made enough for a living that year but not much more.

The following year, before the grapes got too big, we planted black-eye peas. They did beautifully, and we made enough money to buy a small tractor to do much of the work that we previously had to do by hand. The next winter we planted about five acres of strawberries, and they did very well. I guess he knew what he was doing, but we could never make enough money to pay all of our bills. I knew this because my father gave me the responsibility of handling the books. Can you imagine a little thirteen-year old with all that responsibility? I would do the best I could all of those years, and I learned how to handle money. This helped me later in life when I was struggling through college. The grapes started to bear, and we made some extra money, so my dad decided to lease thirty acres across the street from our little farm. Looking back, I realized that was a mistake because that soil was really poor, and it was only suited for pasture, but my dad tried to farm it as he did the other farm to no avail and much expense.

It just wore us down physically, mentally, and financially. That was the year my father became ill and, in my opinion, the added burden led to his death on December 29, 1952. As I said goodbye to him, I remember how well he treated the people who worked for him and the understanding that he had for others. He proved to the many residents and friends that he could do it his way. More about the work on our little farm later in the book.

I left with my friend for San Jose that cold winter morning never to see my father alive again. It was later that morning, during registration, that I heard my named paged over the loud speaker in the men's gymnasium "Calling Julius Manrique," "Calling Julius Manrique," it blared out. I rushed to the office, and the attendant told me to call home immediately because there was an emergency. I went to my apartment with much apprehension and afraid of the worst happening. I called home, and my brother answered. He said Dad died on the way to the hospital this morning about nine o'clock. I almost went into shock not knowing what to do. I immediately made arrangements to go home since the burden of taking care of my mother and three brothers fell upon me. I was the oldest of the four younger ones. I went to the admissions office and dropped all of my classes because I just knew I couldn't do both with this awesome burden placed upon my shoulders. We were in debt, and I knew it. We owed the feed company for various supplies, and we owed the grocery store because we purchased all of our groceries on credit. How could I even think about school with those burdens?

The cost of the burial for my father was shared by the family. My oldest sister's husband took care of all the arrangements, and they were very gracious about it. Somehow the family pulled together during this crisis, and we got through this period. I continued working with the small farm because my father willed it to the four boys. We continued to work the farm as we did when he was living. My brothers went to school and helped me when they came home after school. I was going to make sure that they finished high school one way or the other.

I just couldn't see how I could go back to school with all of these problems and debts. I turned to faith and mental discipline to help me through these adversities. Somewhere, somehow, I could complete my education, help my mother and brothers, and keep the farm going. We decided after a year to give up the lease on the farm that my dad had leased and concentrate on the twenty-seven acres of grapes to which we had clear title. Once we developed a routine there and we were able to complete the tasks that it took to run the vineyard, I re-enrolled at San Jose State. On the weekends I would come home and encourage my brothers to finish high school. They were young, and I'm sure they wanted to quit and go to work somewhere to help with the debts and just have a little money in their pockets. I must have sounded like a broken record, but I just pounded in the idea it would be terrible if they quit, and it would really hurt Mother if they did. I was very happy when the two younger ones finished about the time I started substitute teaching at Oakdale High School where they were enrolled.

I found it very hard to concentrate and get back into the routine, so my grades suffered during the next few quarters. I was living on five dollars a week for groceries and I was paying ten dollars a month for rent. These were times that really tried my soul, heart, and disposition. I couldn't make "B' grades until I took a music course from a very fine instructor. I had to take a music appreciation course for my credential, so I took an elementary voice class. All of our family enjoyed singing because it was a characteristic we inherited from our grandparents and my mother. This instructor must have sensed my troubled soul and took me aside and said, "You know, young man, you have a wonderful voice, but you have to shed some tears. While you sing, go ahead—that's good for you." I did go to the practice room on her advice and shed a lot of tears until I could sing the song or songs without them. I practiced and practiced until I was ready to do my solo. When it was my turn to sing this religious song as a solo for the class, the tears began to roll down my checks, and I believe the class understood because either she had prepared them or just knew this was a good catharsis for me. She was a truly understanding person, and I really enjoyed the class so much that I repeated it the following semester. I was the only non-music major in her advanced voice music class, and I sang along with the best of them. I knew that I could never be an outstanding singer, but I could enjoy the wonderful feeling of singing those various songs. This helped me tremendously, and my grades began to show it. How essential it is for teachers and professors to recognize and realize the impact they have upon students they face each day and that imparting their knowledge isn't the only thing that is necessary in the classroom. I had little time for play while at college, but I made time for my music. I did not join one club or organization while I was in college—no time, no money. I had only three goals while I lived in San Jose-staying alive, getting my teaching credential, and obtaining a bachelor's degree.

8. Sidetracked

Somehow time passed by quickly. The year slipped by. However, another crisis was about to happen to me. During the early summer days, while working in the cannery, I hurt my back lifting fruit cans on a machine that filled the cans with syrup. The pain started out very slowly with a pain in my leg and then spread to the lower part of my back. Again, being ignorant of various types of physical problems, I thought that I was out of shape and started to exercise more. Well, that just caused further pain. Also, as in the case of my father, we did not have any health insurance, so we just didn't go to the doctor until it was very late. I had heard that chiropractors could help, so I went to one in Oakdale. If I were to do it again, I would strongly advise against them working on this type of ailment. He actually led me astray and probably caused more harm than good. I had several adjustments with this person; it was a terrible experience. He told me that I had one leg shorter than the other, so he prescribed one shoe to be built up, and I wore that for some time. No help at all! After almost passing out on the table during an adjustment, I never went back to him.

While at school one morning, I rushed to get out of bed, and I really wrenched something in the lower part of my back. I couldn't stand up straight or even walk well. Good thing it was a Friday, and I somehow made it to classes that day. Afterwards, my friend let me lie in the back seat as we drove home. I went to my family doctor, and he diagnosed the problem immediately. I had ruptured a disc or two in the lumbar region, and he recommended traction or surgery immediately. This was too much to take, and I really didn't know what to do. I talked it over with my oldest sister who lived in San Francisco and who had worked in a hospital. She was familiar with all kinds of illnesses, so somehow she managed to get me into the University of California hospital clinic. Several months later I made my way into the hospital for further examinations. Yes, I had injured several discs, and the doctors also recommended surgery. I was afraid because in those days the success rate for laminectomies was not that good. I said no because I wanted to finish my college degree first just in case something really went wrong. They then put me in a cast from my neck to my hip to immobilize the movements of my back. I wore this to school and at work for six months. It helped a little so the doctors decided to use a steel brace, which would give me a little air circulation around my body, and I could take it off when I bathed and slept. This helped tremendously, but when I took it off, the pain returned in my leg and lower back. Therefore, I wore the brace for three years until I got my credential and degree. That was in the middle of the school year of January 1956.

I was physically a mess, so I returned to Oakdale to recuperate and just relax. I didn't have the strength to look for a job, so I decided to wait until the spring to do that. While at home, my neighbor came by and asked if I wanted to substitute teach. There was a real need for substitutes at the local high school. I went to the local high school and introduced myself to the principal. He was an ex-officer from the Navy, and it appeared everyone addressed him "Yes, sir!" I was neat and clean so that must have impressed him, and he gave me a job. I was teaching all subjects there at the high school for eighteen dollars a day! Can you imagine that? At the end of the month, I received a check in the mail for my services—my first job from my education had just born some fruit, from my mother's garden.

After four and one half years of pain, suffering, heart aches, death in the family, dropping out of school, hurting my back and other adversities, I finally saw the end of the tunnel and the possible financial rewards of an education. How could I possibly encourage others to do the same? How could I ask and persuade others of my heritage to sacrifice almost everything in order to obtain a college education and degree? I cashed my first check and opened up a savings account immediately. I made up my mind at that point that I was never going to be broke, poor, ill or down and out again the rest of my life. I was going to enjoy some of the fruits of my labor and do some of the things the "others" have done for many years. As a substitute, I taught almost all the disciplines at the high school and I had a wonderful time. The students were great, and they seemed to enjoy my mannerisms and teaching. Keep in mind I was just five or six years older than some of the seniors.

Later, while I was substituting at an elementary school, the superintendent offered me my first contract. This was the same superintendent whom I met when there was a break in my education, and I was looking for a teaching job on a provisional credential several years earlier. I went to his home north of town and knocked on his door. He recognized me but was rather surprised to see me. I said I was looking for a job, and his immediate reply was that he did not have any custodial jobs available. I was rather shocked at that but somehow I muttered, no, I was looking for a teaching position. He regained his composure and said that there were no positions available, and I left. Now, he offered me a position as an eight-grade social studies teacher. In retrospect, I guess this was one reason I remained in Oakdale so long so I could remind him that I was equipped mentally and educationally to teach alongside any Anglo teachers whom he hired at very low pay. I signed my first contract for the sum of four thousand dollars. That was more money than my father made in two years and more money than I ever had in my life up to that point.

During the summer of 1956 I made a decision to have a laminectomy, because the brace really had been hampering my teaching and participation in various activities. I went into the University of California Hospital for surgery on June 18 and spent two weeks recuperating. It was my first and only time in the hospital and flat on my back. According to my oldest sister who visited me every day, it was touch and go for many hours because of my poor physical condition. I had some complications and severe problems and I was in the recovery room longer than expected. The doctor told my sister that I looked like a fifty-year-old man, and yet, I was only twenty-three years old. All the pain, stress, worry and problems had taken their toll on my body since the loss of my father in 1952. After about eighteen days, I felt great and was released from the hospital. I was told if any problems occurred to come back. I was a lucky one for I never had any problems, nor did I ever return to that hospital. I have thanked them many times over and over again for the great job that they did!

9. My First Teaching Year

I went home and recuperated for the rest of the summer. A few exercises here and there, but not ones too strenuous, were prescribed by the doctors. I put the steel brace in the closet and felt like a new man. I started my first year of teaching in the fall of 1956, and I never looked back or ever wanted to change my career. This is what I had worked for all of those years, and I was going to be the best teacher the students ever had every year. I knew what not to do to students because of all the experiences I had growing up and the various good and poor teachers that I had. I believe we all do things from the experiences that we have when we are younger. My formative education was taught by so many poor teachers who really, in my opinion, should not have been in the classroom.

I immediately hit it off very well with the students for many reasons. I liked being around these young people, and they sensed it. My first teaching year just zipped by. The students learned, and I learned from them. I taught social studies in the departmentalized system, which meant that mathematics, science, art, English, etc. were taught by someone else. When I corrected the papers, I corrected every possible mistake or error on them. I always gave two written grades, one for content and one for accuracy. I corrected spelling, punctuation, thought process, and made comments on each paper. I would give several classroom assignments each week that each student had to complete. The class was well organized so students knew exactly what to expect each and every day. Students knew that the material that they took home to study and prepare was important to the smooth function of the class the next day or week or month. Everyone was expected to contribute to the discussion and learning processes of the class. I had five periods of thirty to thirty-eight students in each class. I didn't have an aide or someone to type my materials and tests. They were prepared by me, and I had the students write, write, and write more each day. Everyone who entered my classroom was important regardless of economic, social, or political background. My classroom was a happy and relaxed one because the students had a major part in the daily operation of it. The students had fun learning to be good citizens and students (many would tell me later that was the best experience they had ever had in school). I poured on the assignments, and the students really responded. One bulletin board in the classroom was assigned to each of the five classes that I taught, and they had the responsibility to put up bulletins, pictures, drawings, current events, local problems and other items that were relevant to the current reading material that we were studying. They were to change these every two to three weeks, and the more often they were changed, the more credit they would receive.

In the eight years that I taught at Oakdale and in the classroom, not one picture or any part of the room was ever defaced or marked. The students respected this room and the environment. This was the room they wanted to be in a least one time during the day. We did things at the eighth-grade level that some juniors or seniors in high school couldn't do. My peers tried some of my techniques, but they couldn't get the same students to respond the way that I could. I have to believe there are many reasons for this. I don't want to berate the profession, but I must admit that there are many people in the profession who shouldn't be there. I could see some of my peers being very false and inconsistent with the students. I learned much about professional jealously the first years of teaching. That's when I decided to ignore these people and do the best job possible.

One technique which I developed, that many of my former students tell me helped them, was public speaking. As a student, I had a difficult time responding to the teachers, partly because I was shy and partly because I was afraid that I would be embarrassed if I gave the wrong answer. I was conditioned to the latter with my experiences in the third grade and with the physical education coach in high school. I had the custodian make me a podium, which I used to hold my lecture notes when I shared information with the class. I demonstrated to each class how to carry on a discussion and how important it was for the listener to listen when a speaker was trying to convey some ideas. Then, I told the class that each student would lead the class in a daily discussion. You can imagine how that went over. There were moans and groans and statements like, "You'll never get me up in front of the class!" Well, I started by selecting a couple of very outgoing and confident students and went over the procedure that I would like them to follow. Each student would have a list of ten to twenty questions for their lessons that day. These leaders would stand at the podium and ask various questions just as the teacher would. As a matter of procedure they would be the teacher of the period having the responsibility to give the correct answer if a follow-up question happened. I was always there as a backup. I would mark in my roll book every time a student responded in the class with a dot next to their names. This record would be kept so the students that didn't respond were either called on by me or the student teacher for the day. This way students heard their voices and contributed to the class discussion. This made every student responsible for his or her actions at all times.

During my entire teaching career, I never had a discipline problem that I couldn't handle, nor did I ever send a student to the office. I felt strongly about good management of the classroom time, and, if a teacher has that characteristic, he/she will not have discipline problems. Another technique I used to bring warmth to the class was giving the students part of the classroom. Each class was assigned a bulletin board, as was mentioned earlier. I had many ideas and suggestion for displays and those students who wished to be part of a committee would meet with me before or after school to develop something specific. In those days all the office had was old white butcher paper; but, boy, did the students really use that up and developed some very clever bulletin board displays. These displays received extra credit but provided more than that. They gave the students the opportunity to be creative, work with a group of students on a project, give and take on the project to be used that period of time, be part of the classroom ownership, and allow other ways students could perform if their grades weren't that great. These projects many times helped some student's grades. I believe that almost everyone in my classes worked on these projects one time or the other during the school year. There was tremendous enthusiasm for these projects and a lot of respect for each other's ideas. These projects served as lessons also for certain topics that were discussed. The authors of those projects would be called upon to discuss them and provide details. They worked on them to make a beautiful learning environment; they also learned much about the project by doing research for fun. The fastest and the slowest student, got equal attention with research projects, room projects, extra assignments, student teacher of the day, listener, etc. The more you expect from students, the more they will deliver, regardless of their intellectual capacity.

I don't remember ever failing students because there were all kinds of opportunities where they could succeed in my classroom. I never put a student in a position where he or she had to retaliate or fight back. I treated students with tender loving care and with the idea that they were respected and important in my classroom. It was my responsibility to see that students had a good day in school and that they learned in the process. My first eight years of teaching just zoomed by, and I was very happy I found something that I enjoyed doing. I did not consider teaching to be work. My health bounced back, and I had never felt better during those early teaching years.

I did not realize how much influence a teacher has over a young student. I would receive telephone calls at home or I would see parents in different settings, and they would tell me how much their son or daughter enjoyed my class and especially the fairness in the classroom and playground. Teachers must be constantly vigilant on being fair and honest to all their students. This applies to students of all ages, for I have also had the experience of teaching and being an administrator at levels from elementary school to the junior college.

10. Adult Scouter

During my second year of teaching two very important events happened to me that determined what I was to do the rest of my life. Both require much elaboration and I'll not take them in order of importance but chronologically. One afternoon two local businessmen asked to see me after school. One was the Chairman of the local Scout Troop 43 (owner of a metal shop business and member of the local Lions Club), and the other was the Scoutmaster of that troop (he had a local insurance company and also a member of the Lions Club). They politely introduced themselves, and we got right down to the business at hand. They wanted me to be their assistant scoutmaster and I really didn't take too long to respond. I consented and never ever regretted that decision. I was a Scout at one time and thoroughly enjoyed the few years of my activities as a boy. I thought since I was single and I had some time on my hands, I could help a little in the area of scouting. I was introduced to the boys as their assistant and immediately felt I could be of some assistance to the scoutmaster. There were many things that he did that I wouldn't have done during the regular meetings, but he was the scoutmaster so I didn't say too much.

One night, and it was one of the very few nights that someone in my hometown ever asked me over for dinner, the scoutmaster asked me over for dinner. I think I could understand that as a single person, but later when I was married I found that difficult to accept. Little did I know that he wanted to step down, and he felt the troop would be in good hands if I took over. Later in the evening he told me this, but this time my response was a little slower. Later in the week I responded affirmatively, and I confess that he and I became very good friends ever since. He was later to repay me with much kindness during another very crucial part of my life—when I ran unsuccessfully for Stanislaus County Superintendent. He was the first to come to my aid when I announced my candidacy and remained a very loyal and helpful friend until his death.

Well, I launched my avocation as a scoutmaster of troop 43. Like most things that I did, I wanted to have the best troop in the council. That was my goal and we set out to accomplish it. I was firmly convinced that scouting helped me and wanted to give something back to scouting and to the community. I took over the troop with about thirty scouts and rapidly built it to over fifty. This was done by letting the boys run their troop and with much training. I took the patrol leaders and the green bar (Senior Patrol Leader, Scribe, Junior Assistant Scoutmasters) on outdoor training sessions. I provided them with reading material, ideas and examples of how to do various activities. We made these positions important and respected so others would strive to be leaders in the troop.

This worked so well that the fathers of two of the boys in the troop asked me if they could be of some assistance. I made one the assistant in charge of transportation, camping, and campsite locations. Our troop camped out one weekend a month, and it was his responsibility to provide for the site, transportation, etc. for that weekend. He did an excellent job and received much satisfaction seeing his two sons grow and also develop a sense of responsibility (one son went on to become Eagle and President of the Council). The other father was assigned as assistant scoutmaster in charge of advancement. His main thrust was to provide merit badge sessions in different areas each month so the boys could pass these merit badges by way of a rotating or cyclical system. He would also have the senior patrol assigned to help the younger boys through the beginning ranks. I would be in charge of the total program for the year. I would sit down with the green bar and, after hours of planning, we would come up with a theme and a goal for each month. These goals would be broken down into four-week periods so the patrol leaders would meet weekly with their patrol to plan for these activities. These activities would be related to the weekly troop meeting, so each patrol or scout would have to be prepared to perform or conduct some part of the meeting. The troop meeting was planned around the monthly theme and camp outs, thereby giving everyone in the troop every opportunity to succeed and have an excellent camp out. All my years as a scoutmaster were done in this manner.

The enthusiasm, interest, motivation, desire, and sheer love to work hard by every member in the troop just blossomed. The proof of this is when we went on district camporees or council camporals. Our troop was recognized as one of the best organized, motivated, disciplined, and managed troops in the council. We would be envied when we marched into camp in full uniform. It was obvious each boy was responsible for his actions, and he knew it. After the camp was set up, the boys then participated with enthusiasm in all the games and activities that were available. We were a very traditional troop, never using charcoal or any type of butane to cook our meals. Either the boys carried in wood, or they scoured the area for it in order to cook their meals. We really roughed it. This paid off when we went into the high Sierras. At the end of each camp, regardless of the color of ribbon we received, the green bar would review what we did well and what we didn't do so well. These were then reviewed with the troop, and we then set out to make improvement for the next camp out, always giving them a goal.

During my six years as a Scoutmaster, I never ever had to discipline a young scout because of many factors. The boys were all treated equally; they were given individual responsibilities; they were encouraged to use their God-given talents; they were respected for their contributions to the troop; they were rewarded through material or physical recognition at Courts of Honor; they were provided training and leadership skill so they could succeed; and their parents were constantly kept informed and involved regarding the activities of the troop. There was tremendous respect for me, and I respected them also. I was always addressed as Mr. Manrique and, during certain jovial periods, the older scouts knew exactly how far they could go. We really had a beautiful troop, and I truly missed the boys when they moved on to college or moved away. I did keep in touch with a few, and one local dentist and I have lunch at least once a year.

There were several highlights during my career as a scoutmaster. The first being my training at a camp called Woodbadge. I spent ten days with other adult scouters in the high Sierras at Huntington Lake near Fresno learning how to be a better scoutmaster by performing similar tasks that were required of the boys. Over one hundred adults were in this camp, and only five dropped out before the period was over. Once we passed that rigorous test, we had to do research on the scouting movement. I typed over one hundred pages on the subject which gave me tremendous insight into the movement. After this was completed, I had to hold several training sessions for other leaders. I was the first leader in the Yosemite Area Council to have received the Woodbadge Award, and I felt like the most qualified scoutmaster in the council. I set out to encourage other leaders to go to this training, and years later the council had over forty qualified Woodbadgers. The council then began to train some woodbadgers locally.

The second highlight was taking twenty Yosemite Area Council scouts to Philmont Scout Ranch in New Mexico. We took a train from Riverbank and headed south to Williams, Arizona. We stopped to see the Grand Canyon—what a magnificent wonder of the world. Then we made our way to Cimarron, New Mexico. We spent ten days at Camp Philmont that was over one hundred and thirty-three thousand acres donated to the National Boy Scouts by Phillips Oil Company of Tulsa, Oklahoma. Then we boarded the train and headed north to Colorado Springs and spent the night at the Air Force Academy. After that, we left for Sacramento, California, then to Stockton and home. This was a wonderful experience for a young budding scoutmaster. I was full of enthusiasm for scouting.

The third highlight was taking sixteen of my scouts to the National Jamboree, which was held at Colorado Springs in 1960. The site was a beautiful one and all the experiences getting there and back were great, but the two years of preparation to go were more important to the boys and me. All sixteen boys that went from our troop had earned Eagle Scout Rank; however, they were not Eagles when the boys decided to go two years earlier. Our troop had a tradition of having Eagles, but in 1958 ten boys said they would like to go to the Jamboree. So the troop committee and the members of the Lions Club decided to help the boys help themselves with various jobs so they could earn money to go. The boys painted numbers on curbs (paint and stencils provided by the Rotary Club), sold fireworks (scouts kept 75% of the profits), picked fruit (scouts kept all of the profits), worked at the local rodeo grounds selling snow cones (Lions Club provided the snow cone machine and scouts who worked were paid an hourly rate after all the expenses were taken care of), collected and recycled newspaper (profit from this was given directly to the boys who worked), and many other jobs too numerous to mention in order to earn the necessary dollars for the trip. Actually the whole community got behind many of the projects and people were calling me asking if they could help.

The enthusiasm was contagious and more boys decided they were going to be Eagles and earn their way for this Jamboree. Every boy who went earned most of the money or all of it. It was wonderful to see these boys blossom into responsible young men. The parents were enthusiastic, the local newspaper pitched in, and the adult leaders were amazed to see how this goal motivated our troop. On May 10, 1960, we had a Court of Honor and eleven boys received their Eagle Rank. This had to be one of the highlights of my life. We had an excellent Court of Honor and, after, a lovely dinner in the cafeteria of our local school. The mothers helped and really did an excellent job. The boys who did not go to the jamboree also earned enough money to go to Camp Bob McBride during the month of June. Everyone in the troop benefited from this goal and at the end of the year we had a good healthy balance in the troop treasury. I felt that the boys were all prepared to have an excellent time in camp and at the national jamboree. These things happened to me in only three years as a scoutmaster. We had enough money in the bank to pay the dues for all the scouts who worked, provided them with Boys Life magazine and re-registered the troop for the next two years. When I turned the troop over to the next leader, there were still four hundred dollars left in the bank. These were the years that I would remember for a long time to come.

Old scoutmasters don't fade away, they just get trapped into doing something else for the scouting program. I held almost every position in adult scouting with the exception of being President of the Council. I guess the only reason I didn't obtain that position was that I didn't play my political cards correctly, and I angered one of the "old boys" who perennially sat on the nomination committee. He kept me from being nominated. At one of the executive meetings, he and another very influential board member were discussing the slate for the following year. I was mentioned for President, but this particular board member said, "No, he is not ready yet." Well, those of you who have been in politics and hear someone say that, you certainly know what it means. This is the sad part of my scouting career because scouts and scouters are supposed to be friendly and honest. When you are trying to do something and introduce change, you can't help but make someone angry, and then that either places labels on you as being rough around the edges or being too aggressive.

It seemed that I was always for the underdog; therefore, I spoke my mind when it came to helping correct an injustice. This council was ruled by a small clique and the executive. When it came to awarding the Silver Beaver (the highest scouting award given to an adult scouter in the council), it was usually given to an individual who was on the executive board and a person who had contributed much money for a particular project. This is understandable, but when it was flagrant, then I felt something had to be done. When I got on the board, I made absolutely sure a more equitable and just system was set up. I helped change the procedure for nominating potential candidates and introduced the idea that women should be selected also. As a matter of fact during my term as Chairman of the Nominating Committee, we selected our first woman for the Silver Beaver (now called the Silver Fawn). Many more scouters who toiled in the trenches would receive the award after my tenure as Chair of that committee.

This individual on the Executive Council was, I thought, a good friend for the past twenty years, but I had mistaken him entirely and he turned against me during the apex of my scouting and political career. Other than that, I had an excellent scouting career gaining the respect of many in the area. I was given the Silver Beaver which is the highest award a council can bestow upon an individual. I was the youngest adult to ever receive the award up to that time in January 1963. I was thirty-one years old. I have received all the awards that can be given an adult with the exception of the regional or national scouting awards and those are given to wealthy and influential people throughout the United States. I know I'll never fall into that category, nor do I feel that I have the political or social influence for the right people to nominate me. One can see how political Scouting becomes once you step out of the scoutmaster's position.

Therefore, the highlight of my scouting career was receiving the Silver Beaver Award. I had worked hard for this because my former scoutmaster received it in 1956, the year I started my teaching career. I said to myself then that he was an excellent choice, and he was a man who deserved it. I wished that some day I could emulate him as a scoutmaster and receive a similar award. Since I received my award, I have helped many deserving scoutmasters receive this award because I have been on many nominating committees. This unwritten policy of giving scoutmasters this award in this council was largely my influence because up until that time only influential people and executive board members who donated large sums of money received the award in this council. Little did I know how political this was and how I was influencing procedures for future potential recipients.

I had been on the executive board for many years, but would not have been nominated because I was a little outspoken as a scoutmaster. The composition of the board was completely white with one exception—me. I was the only Mexican-American on it, and I felt accepted only because of my strong enthusiasm, knowledge, experience and background in scouting. Other members were there because of their social, political and economic positions, and that helps them with their businesses. That is understandable because, without the movers or shakers, many of these community activities would not exist. My enthusiasm for Scouting was dampened very much in 1978 when one of these scouters who I thought was a friend supported another candidate for office rather than remaining neutral. It hurt me seriously because up until that time I had strong convictions about people in general and never distrusted anyone. I guess looking back over my scouting career I could have been considered a little naive and idealistic. This incident modified my attitude and philosophy about people and my desire to help at the community level.

11. My Father's Birthplace

The second, and most important event, that happened to me during the second year of teaching was that I managed to save a few dollars to enroll in an extension course offered by Stanford University at Mexico City College in Mexico, City. This was my first opportunity to travel south of Bakersfield and out of the country. When I left home that summer and traveled to Los Angeles by train through the San Joaquin Valley, I could not believe some of the things that I saw—both wonderful and depressing. When I entered Tijuana, Mexico on my way to the airport, I was thoroughly amazed. The poverty that existed in that area was something I had never seen even though our family was considered poor. This was a sight I was never to forget, and it helped me coin a phrase, "Si, se puede" Yes, you can do it. This was in 1957 before the phrase was used by many people. I don't claim ownership of the words because many different nationalities use it in one way or the other, but I just knew that I would have to overcome my deficiencies. Strive for whatever you aim for and complete it with satisfaction barring severe health problems.

As we boarded the airplane, I met several individuals, and we talked all the way to Mexico City. I had made arrangements for room and board through the college, but I arrived too late in the evening to drive to the boarding house. So, I spent my first night in Mexico City in a beautiful hotel. I should probably state that all of these experiences were to be a first for me because of my poor economic and social background. The following day was Sunday, and a friend whom I met on the airplane and I had breakfast in the coffee shop of the hotel. Shortly after, two Americans approached us and asked us for help with a camera. We helped them and they asked if we had plans for the day. We didn't, and they asked us to join them. We spent the entire day with them driving in and around Mexico City. The time just passed so quickly as we moved from one historical monument to the other. We had a wonderful day with them and later had a glorious dinner. They lived in Los Angeles and were on vacation. They were to continue on with other activities, and we went our way. I corresponded with them for a few years after, but then lost contact with them. What a nice couple to offer us their friendship and the use of their car for the day. This was a period of the "Ugly American," and many of the natives felt that we were intruders and all very wealthy.

Mexico City College was located on a ridge overlooking a large valley in one of the loveliest parts of Mexico City. This particular class was sponsored by Stanford University under the direction of one of their Professor, Dr. Ronald Hilton. The class lectures were on Mondays, Wednesdays, and Fridays. Tuesdays and Thursdays were reserved for field trips or excursions on our own. We all decided on a topic for a research paper and proceeded to collect data on it. Part of the project had to be accomplished through interviews with businessmen, engineers, doctors, lawyers, teachers, and people on the street. I was so impressed with the geography of the country that I decided to write on the development of Mexico City. This was quite a project, and I narrowed it down to a specific area of the city. I had a great time using my Spanish that had been dormant all these years. My father did not teach us Spanish because he wanted us to learn English first. He was a firm believer that if you are going to live and work in the United States you had better learn the language so you could communicate in that language. He spoke Spanish to my mother, but like the majority of the Mexican-American families of my era, the children grew up without really learning it. I learned it while picking peaches with the "nationals" or "wetbacks," as they were called during my youth. I learned rapidly because there was a need to. I continued to study in high school and college until I was very accurate and bilingual.

While doing research for my project, I interviewed professors, engineers, and businessmen. The most impressive Mexican I interviewed was the man who designed the forty-two storey Latin American building in Mexico City, the highest building built at that time—1957. The building is an engineering feat and would be one of the wonders of the world. Because of its design, it can withstand the tremendous earthquakes that occur frequently in Mexico. Many people don't know that Mexico City is located in a valley over a mile high in altitude. In 1957 when I was there, it was virtually free from smog, but when I returned nineteen years later, it was difficult for me to breathe the air because it was so polluted. Many times I would have to use a handkerchief to help filter the air I was breathing. I assumed this was all in the name of progress.

Well, during my many adventures in Mexico City, I met the student body president of Hope College, Holland Michigan. We became good friends and he asked, "What are your plans for the next year?" I replied, "I have none." He indicated that a similar program would be offered by Hope College in Vienna, Austria, next year. I didn't give this much thought then because of the expense involved in a trip, and I thought a lowly paid schoolteacher couldn't afford a trip like that.

The ten weeks just zoomed by during that summer because of the interesting classes and the trips that we took. I spent a long four-day weekend on the beaches of Vera Cruz eating fresh pineapples and bananas. The roaches and bugs got into our blankets while we slept on the beaches like beach bums, but being flexible and youthful we ended up sleeping on and in the car. When it rained, we did what the natives did, just ignored it and went on with our business.

Another very exciting trip was to Acapulco, in the Western part of Mexico. Four of us rented a car and drove the distance without sleeping. We rented a hotel room and took turns cleaning up the place. This was a beautiful site and setting that overlooked the bay. Our weekend was interrupted by a strong earthquake, which did a lot of damage to the hotel, airport, roads, etc. We were stranded in this lovely city for four extra days because the roads were too damaged, and no one could use them. I had much trepidation regarding all of my personal belongings in Mexico City since we had heard over the radio that much of the city was completely destroyed. After the roads were opened, we made our way back to Mexico City. We saw the destruction and damage done by Mother Nature—it was rather incomprehensible and, yet, we survived. The drive back was much slower because there were many detours.

Finally, we arrived in Mexico City about 1 a.m., and we really didn't see any major damage. The next day as I walked around the city. It was a very different story. One building which really impressed me, in 1957 was the Hilton Hotel, located on the Paseo de la Reforma which I walked by dozens of times. The earthquake damaged it severely. On my second trip to Mexico City, I looked for this hotel as a landmark but could not fine it. I asked the taxi cab driver what had happened and he gave me a long story which I did not verify, but something like this happened. This Hilton chain asked that the engineers and architects be held responsible for the damages to their property and sued for damages. Although many individuals lost their jobs for the poor construction, the Hilton chain could not get the government to pay for the damages to this beautiful hotel. The cab driver said the Hilton chain just moved all of their hotels out of Mexico. I mention this for two reasons—money talks and governments can make some big mistakes.

I had always walked to almost every spot I went in Mexico City and learned so much in the process. The transportation system was very economical and it was a learning experience. I was able to communicate with the natives which really enhanced my trips. I spent a long weekend visiting my father's brother and two sisters in Leon, Guanajuato. It was a lengthy and tedious trip north of Mexico City which consisted of about three hundred miles traveling in a Greyhound bus. The bus drivers certainly had fun negotiating the narrow cobblestone streets of the small villages that we went through, The main streets had adobe buildings on both sides and, at two or three o'clock in the morning, the bus driver would make the bus howl by shifting gears and double clutching at every turn in order to make more noise and just maybe wake somebody up. It was interesting to watch the drivers when they changed gears and gunned the engine as to tell the campesinos, "Watch out, here I come!" They took pride in their jobs and made sure the country folks knew they were coming.

We arrived in Leon about six o'clock in the morning and the city was just waking up. We checked into the hotel and then dropped off for a little sleep. You didn't dare go to sleep on the bus because you would miss all the action of the countryside, and the discussion that went on between the bus driver and various passengers. After a shower, my friend went his way, and I went to meet my relatives. My father had talked about his family, but only in generalities. I saw one aunt who was living in a small room above a church, and we talked at some length. Later, she gave me the directions to find her sister and brother. I made my way to the outskirts of the city to seek out my father's relatives. I finally found one family in a very poor section of town—we would call it a "barrio." I talked with them all that day and then returned the following day for more. In the meantime, I met my uncle who had visited us in the United States several years before. He thought our standard of living was in the wealthy class compared to theirs. Our discussion went on and on and, during this period, I really got a deep insight why the camposinos leave their country seeking jobs, any types of jobs, in the United States. They would work for almost nothing and live in hovels or sleep on the ground in the United States, and it would be better than what some of them had. My first-hand education here was something I would never forget. It is ironic that so many leave their families and head north to be taken advantaged of, abused, denigrated, berated, scorned, detested, and treated like animals for doing the hardest and lowliest labor that exists in the United States. Large groups of the regular American labor force complain bitterly about "these people" taking jobs, but many of these same people have grown so soft on social welfare benefits that they wouldn't even think of doing this kind of labor. Oh, how my eyes watered to see how humans treat their fellow humans of a different color and, yet, these wealthy farmers and businessmen sleep well at night after making a profit from the sweat and blood of the poor peasants. This brought back memories of how my father walked the well-beaten path across the border at Texas up to the state of Colorado. There he spent many cold and bitter years until he made his way to California to seek a better way of life like so many before and after him had done. There the climate was similar to Leon, and there he met my mother and settled down. Thank goodness we were instilled with pride to work hard for a day's pay and never to steal, borrow, or take anything without repaying it. Yes, as I visited my cousins and other relatives I could visualize why my father had left this country. There was no way in his lifetime he could rise above his preordained station in life there. The rich got richer, and the poorer got poorer. This was the tune during his lifetime and continued until his death in 1952. I vowed that this would not happen to me, and I would remember what he said over and over again—Si, se puede! I used that phrase as a philosophy all my life and encouraged my students and other Mexican-Americans to do the same. There are many successful Mexicans in the country, but they are a very small a percentage in relation to the greater population in the U.S.

After my brief stay in Leon, I made my way back to Mexico City with experiences and first-hand knowledge of my father's past. I just wished I had more time to explore the library and records of his family, but that would have to wait for another time. My ten weeks in Mexico were coming to a close, and I completed my project and turned it in. I lived in a flat with two elderly women who rented out bedrooms to the college. This income was enough to support them and to have a "criada" (a poor Indian maid from the countryside) help them. During my many breakfasts and dinners in that household, I learned that other countries have their prejudices and biases also. They treated the "Indios" (Indians) just as bad as some Americans treated Mexicans, American Indians, and blacks. These two women treated this maid with contempt and made her work very hard. I don't know if this was typical but I had heard this was prevalent in Mexico. The darker the skin, the more difficult time a person had. We had some very good discussions, and I'm sure when I left they had a different impression of me and the United States.

12. Summer of 1957

When I returned from Mexico the summer of 1957, a friend called and asked if I wanted to tour the United States. I was broke, but what an opportunity! I borrowed some money, washed my clothes and off across the county we went, sharing expenses with his car. As we drove across this big, beautiful, fortunate and prosperous country, we compared it to the country south of the border. We visited cities such as Salt Lake City, Utah; Cheyenne, Wyoming; Lincoln, Nebraska; Sioux City, Iowa; Chicago, Illinois; Lansing, Michigan; Gary, Indiana; Niagara Falls, New York; New York, New York; Baltimore, Maryland; Washington, D.C.; Raleigh, North Carolina; Atlanta, Georgia; Opelika, Alabama; New Orleans, Louisiana; Houston, Texas; Dallas, Texas; Albuquerque, New Mexico; Phoenix, Arizona; and many cities in California on the way back to Oakdale, California, after the trip. This was truly a trip for me to remember, and I had many delightful experiences along the way. I could not get over how large our country was and the enormous potential and wealth that existed. I felt proud to be an American of Mexican descent and displayed this everywhere I went. I am still proud, but the more one reads about individuals who were supposed to be examples and models to follow, the harder it is to really be enthusiastic about many of the things that this country has done. The Watergate scandal when a President was called a crook and stood before millions of people denying it—this was a low point in my belief in some leaders. Being a Californian, I knew all about this president and his political background. In my opinion, next to the movie actor that was a president he was the worst one that I could remember. Many people in this country knew all about this man's background but went ahead and voted him into office because down deeply they too had some of these same characteristics. The Vietnam War and the whole political affair during the sixties when the American people were just lied to, over and over again, was a period of my life when I just about lost faith in our country. I have realized, since that day, that the backbone of our country is the average, well-informed citizen. When officials who are in leadership positions lie to the average citizen, then the foundation of our country begins to shake and crumble. We must never let situations like this happen again because we really have a fine democratic country. It appears that people all over the world want to come to the United States and pay dearly to do so. Many of these immigrants want a better life for themselves and especially for their children. The United States is still the mecca for individuals, for the oppressed and poor. As I traveled on my trip across the country, I met and talked to Midwesterners, New Englanders, Southerners, and tourists from all parts of the world. I found out that people are basically the same with similar aspirations and desires. I learned first hand the prejudices that some people harbored, and these prejudices are emitted when one's livelihood or social status is threatened. As I traveled through the South, I found restrooms for "whites" and for "blacks." A very real line appeared where the "blacks" were to be in the South in 1957. This was several years after the Warren Court decision on the "Brown vs. Topeka" case outlawing separate but equal educational facilities. The more I analyzed the situation, I realized all the prejudices and inhuman acts that occurred are done by individual people. In order to get at the root of these problems, you had to educate them. When you educate people, then you create other dilemmas. For example, if I hadn't the opportunity for an education, I wouldn't have been able to teach and travel to see first hand the many things that existed in this country. I remembered my mother always telling me to smile a little more, but I couldn't because I knew that so many unfortunate people were starving, being humiliated and dying throughout the world. My mother was quite a woman, regardless of the poverty and her lack of formal education. It appeared she was always happy and positive.

She had quite a philosophy, but probably never knew the word. She never cheated, lied, distrusted, or disliked anyone all during her lifetime. I do remember a little white lie she told on my behalf. I remember coming home from school one day, and we passed by a home that had several orange trees. Each year we would see those oranges fall on the ground and rot. The owner never seemed to care.

Well, this friend and I jumped over the fence and grabbed a few. Just at that time the owner came out and shouted at us. We took off like scared rabbits, and he chased us all the way home which was about four blocks. I ran into the house and hid under the bed. A few minutes later that man was pounding on the door and shouting to my mother that he wanted to see that little thief who was stealing his oranges. My mother politely said that her boys don't steal and closed the door in his face. I got an ear-full from my mother that night, and I don't believe I ever "lifted" anything else in my life after that experience. We never went by that house again, and I never took a thing from anyone the rest of my life. As a result of that experience, later in life, when we purchased a home in Modesto, our front and back yard had thirteen citrus trees, plus a peach, pear, apple, and almond tree. Also we had grapes and berries. I shared these with my brothers, sisters, friends, neighbors and students at school. So, instead of letting the fruit rot, I made sure other people enjoyed them also. I gave away boxes of fruit to the Gospel Mission, Inter-faith ministries, Salvation Army, students and neighbors as a result of that miserly old man who chased me home because I attempted to take one orange from his trees. Every year, when I make my rounds giving this fruit away, I think of that person and his greed.

13. Summer of 1958

When our trip concluded, after twenty-one days on the road across the United States, I started my second year of teaching with much enthusiasm. I had visited a foreign country and traveled through thirty-six states. I was loaded with experiences that would enrich my teaching for many years to come. I shared these experiences with my students and community. I spoke and sang to groups at every occasion. I wanted to let the people know about our country, and I shared my time with them generously. The second year of teaching was as smooth as the first, and I really enjoyed it. I helped with the honor society, student body, and coached a basketball team for almost no pay. I felt that this was what teachers were expected to do, and so I did it unselfishly. Little did I know that many years later, the "profession" would bargain dollars for each of the these activities and require that teachers make a decent wage for their services as it should have been. The profession in my opinion deteriorated after California foolishly passed Proposition 13 in 1978 The California school system went from the top-ranked system to the bottom in a matter of a few years. This started a trend for the field of education in state after state. As funding became tight, more money was spent on prisons than on education.

But it was in the fall of 1957 when I wrote to a history professor at Hope College, Holland, Michigan. That letter lead to the next greatest event in my life which firmly instilled in my mind my personal philosophy "si, se puede." I inquired about their summer school program that was to be held in Vienna, Austria. He responded quickly and sent me all the applications necessary for the trip. I replied and started to save for this trip. I read about this country and parts of Europe that we were to visit. The adrenaline began to flow profusely just thinking about the trip and that it would be possible for me to make such a journey. There were members on the staff that were near retirement and they had not been out of the country. How could a second-year teacher—a poor Mexican at that—afford to make this trip? This is mentioned because I was the only Mexican-American teacher on the staff, and I was the first native-born Mexican-American hired in Stanislaus County. In many respects, this county was very prejudiced and biased towards minorities. There has never been a Mexican-American elected to a high position in the county government, nor has there been a Mexican-American County Superintendent of Schools. Only in the late sixties and early seventies, because of federal money, projects and affirmative action, were Mexicans allowed in the classrooms in this county and some parts of the state. There were Hispanic teachers in the county i.e. Guatemalans, Costa Ricans, Cubans, and Puerto Ricans, but no native born Mexican- American. Later in this story I will give you some more insight on how lonely it was to be the only Mexican-American administrator at the elementary, secondary and college level, but for now, we will continue with my planned trip to Europe.

I had never been away on an extended trip before (other than the trip across the United States and to Mexico). This trip was to be for almost three months. I started to plan for the trip by going to the library and checking out reading material and German records in order to learn a little of the language. I began learning to speak German. That was a new experience for me. I played the records hour after hour and slowly began to learn the language. I would practice it on my mother and she would laugh. I would come home from teaching and greet her in German—and she would say, "cut it out, it sounds funny." I would learn the language so well that I gave directions in German to the natives while I was in Austria with the fullest confidence. June rolled around, and I left school a day early in order to fly from San Francisco to New York and then to Montreal, Quebec, where we would board the SS Arcadia for our trip to Europe. The flight was exhilarating, and I just couldn't believe I was making this journey. When I boarded the ship in Montreal and met the rest of the contingent, it just was too hard for me to believe. I immediately took a liking to the director because he was a humble, shy, honest, and intelligent man. We established a friendship that would last for many years. I was introduced to many of the other students and felt very comfortable with the group. I was later to share a flat in Vienna with a person from Lansing, Michigan. The director of the tour paired the students off and placed us in homes throughout the city near the University. As the ship pulled away from the dock, there was the usual confetti and the waving of hands from relatives and friends of people aboard the ship. It was a lovely sight as we slipped under the huge bridges that span the St. Lawrence River and I wondered how the French settlers came up and down this river without the power that this ship had. I rarely stayed in my cabin because where was too much to see and do on deck. Many times I would stand at the stern and say to myself—is this really happening to me, a person from a little town in California making this trip to a place that was only in the history or geography books? In Vienna, I developed a love for that city that will last me a lifetime.

The S.S. Arcadia was a beautiful 25,000-ton Greek liner with a German captain, Spanish crew and Italian orderlies. The accommodations were fine for me, but some of the other "spoiled brats," as I later found out, complained bitterly. The food was excellent, and on two occasions I dined with the captain because I had performed at a couple of church services for the recreational group on board. I participated in many activities on the ship that gave me the opportunity to meet many people. Please keep in mind, at that time I was a very shy and reserved individual, but on some occasions I would try different things and break out of my shell. The events on the ship were well planned and I enjoyed every minute of the trip except when we went through a tremendous storm. Somehow my digestive system survived that, but that of many people didn't. They got seasick and remained either in their rooms or in sick bay. After seven wonderful days, we landed in Cherbourg, France, during the early hours of the morning. We were greeted by a Mercedes-Benz, air-conditioned, thirty-five passenger bus. We all boarded it along with our luggage and off we went through Cherbourg, heading for Paris. This was the beginning of a fourteen-day bus tour to Paris, Bruges, Brussels, Amsterdam, Bonn, Heidleburg, Passau and finally Vienna, Austria. Those fourteen days gave me the opportunity to use my German, Spanish and a few phrases in the French language that I had been studying for the past few months. I guess the most important part of a trip is the planning of one. Reading about the castles, monuments, rivers, products, and the people was really the essential part of the trip. Unfortunately, I didn't do much of this before this trip; however, I did learn a lot first hand. One learns by osmosis if the exposure is great enough. I always kept this in mind when I was teaching. When you provide an environment of learning for the student, they can't help but learn even if they cannot read. I learned so much about people, cultures, geography and politics of Europe in 1958. I walked everywhere in Europe and I had a chance to meet and greet people, as well as I could, in their language. Please keep in mind we were still known as the Ugly American since it had not been too long after World War II. I talked to the common person on the street, in the stores, post offices, opera house, etc. People were safe on the streets at all hours of the night and day. It was beautiful meeting people at all hours of the day. I guess being single made it easy for me to do many of the things I did, and I had few inhibitions during that period of my life. Later, during my married life, this whole attitude changed because I didn't feel as comfortable or as free to make mistakes in the presence of my family.

My educational experiences continued to broaden each day while I was in Europe. I was eager to meet and learn something on every occasion. It is a little unfortunate that this zeal is lost when some individuals age and become more secure with their lives. The excursion took us to Brussels, the site of the 1958 World's Fair. I had never been to a "fair" of this magnitude in my whole life. I remembered when the World's Fair was located on Mare Island in the middle of the bay between Oakland and San Francisco in 1939. I remembered because I was in the fourth grade and the teacher announced that, if we had fifty cents, a bus would take the children to see it. We also had to bring a sack lunch, but my family didn't have the money, or we didn't know what a sack lunch was because all we ate at that time were tacos. San Francisco was only ninety miles away, but it could have been 4,000 miles away for all I knew of the distance. It was impossible for me to go, and I remembered shedding some tears after asking my mother and her reply was we could not afford it. No, we couldn't afford it, and my dad wouldn't let me go because I was needed to help on the weekends. These thoughts came back to me as I stood underneath this huge atomium, the centerpiece of the 1958 World Fair. These gigantic spheres were eighty feet in diameter and an escalator ran through each of them. I was overwhelmed with this structure and all the other huge displays that were there. Another outstanding feature that remained vividly in my mind was the European Economic Community building. This was the foundation of the Common Market of Europe which made the continent very wealthy economically much later. We took a tour through the mock underground coal mine, and I met a very bright tour guide who could speak nine languages including Spanish. After the tour, we had coffee and we conversed in Spanish for some time. She was Flemish and as a young girl had command of French, German, Flemish, and Belgian. She later learned the other five languages plus English. The more languages she knew the more she was paid as a tour guide. From there we made our way to Amsterdam and the Hague—The International Court of Justice. This was a sight to behold. I just couldn't believe I was there watching this very important body working. I wish now that I had made notes of all these experiences, but if I had I would have had volumes to carry around. We then moved up along the Rhine River towards Bonn. I took great notice of the geography of the country and learned much about the agricultural products of Europe. The manner in which the grapes are grown on the slopes intrigued me. How the farmers placed rocks on the ground to prevent erosion was amazing. I was amazed to see such lovely vineyards and farms. The country side with its lush crops and healthy looking animal stock. So, so different from where I lived and it should have been because I was eight thousand miles away and lived at different latitude. The Rhine River was like a highway with the barges moving in both directions like the lumbering diesel trucks which move the products up and down highways "99" and "5" in California. The major difference was the beauty of the river and the efficiency of this mode of transportation in Europe. Their railroads ran on time, and they were great movers of people and products. Everything seemed to be planned for effective use of resources and for the ultimate benefit of the people.

We stopped at Heidelberg located on the Neckar River. I was so exhausted that day; I left the group that was going on a tour and made my way to a park along the river. It was a beautiful sunny day, and I decided just to sit and talk to people as they walked by. Later in the afternoon, I fell asleep along the bank of the river. I must have slept four or five hours undisturbed. I joined the group for dinner, and then we toured the city. The next day we moved on to Passau and then the long drive to Vienna, Austria. Much of Austria is mountainous, but the farmers utilize every piece of farmable acreage. All kinds of crops are grown, but in small quantities. The farms are meticulous, and the barns are kept up as well as their homes. The neatness and verdant areas were quite a contrast from the farmers in California. We entered Vienna during a thunderstorm in the late afternoon. Our entrance lay in the direction of the Black Forest. It was rainy and cold. I became accustomed to this weather during my eight-week stay there, and my German language was really put to good use. The director placed me with another student of my age, in a flat on the Schonbrun Strasse, near the Schonbrun Palace. We became very good friends during our stay, but we didn't see much of each other. The daily schedule was a continental breakfast provided by the house frau, which consisted of a tasty cup of coffee and a hot roll and jelly. We had lunch at the University family style, so you could eat all you wanted, and, then, for dinner we ate in various restaurants in the city. The director would reimburse us five dollars a week so we could use our language for ordering meals. The latter was truly a memorable experience. A group of us would try different restaurants almost every night of the week. Remember at that time the dollar was worth four to one during the late fifties, so we really had some buying power. My classes consisted of the history of Germany and music appreciation. The history was taught by a native German, and we learned a lot more that what was in the book from him. The music class was more than I bargained for. We were required to attend concerts that were delightful, especially when the director provided the tickets for us. On these occasions, we would attend the open-air concerts in the folk parks of our choice. These were held on different schedules throughout the summer at no cost to anyone. We really soaked up the music and culture that summer.

14. Lovely Vienna

I met three wonderful women in Vienna. Two were to give me a tremendous lesson in understanding people even though there was a language problem, and the other was to become my wife after four years of communicating with her by mail. The first was a Czechoslovakian who worked as a secretary in Vienna, a beautiful and bright woman whom I respected immediately. I met her at a dance in the Volkspark one evening. My German improved tremendously especially when we dated frequently. I guess I was a little old fashioned and I had learned much from my mother. She reminded me to treat other women like your sister. That didn't leave me much room to get into trouble. This probably sounds a little corny, but it was firmly instilled in my mind, and I did treat the women I dated with respect. We dated on several occasions, and she showed me this lovely city from a different perspective which I would have never experienced otherwise. I guess the one moment that I remember the most was when we took a trip up this huge ferris wheel—I understand it is the largest in the world. As it made its way around the arc, she pointed out all the landmarks of the city. During the end of my stay there, I rushed around for a couple of days taking pictures of those landmarks and other sights of the city. I was careful never to carry a trench coat or a camera during my stay there because this was a dead give away for recognition of a tourist. Vienna really came alive as we took the streetcars to all parts of the city. We walked through park after park seeing the statues of the great music masters. The buildings were more than buildings; they were history, traditions, faith, and the cultures of these people. It was something that I would try to instill in the minds of my students when I returned to teaching in the fall. I very much wanted to pursue our relationship further, but I knew we had a cultural difference and, besides, if we did get serious, she would be over ten thousand miles away from home—that would be a very expensive trip to take once or twice a year. I learned that people are similar throughout the world regardless of the color of their skin and their nationality. We all have feelings and usually are willing to accept other people's points of view until something drastic happens. The night I left Vienna I cried because I really had fallen in love with the city and its people. She and a friend came to bid us farewell, and I just about got off the train to stay, but my better judgment told me not to. The train pulled out of the station, and many vivid and wonderful memories were left behind. I would think and talk about that wonderful city the rest of my life.

The house frau was also another person I really got to know. I spent many afternoons and late evenings talking to her in German. She was a woman in her sixties with a very fine and warm personality. She reminded me so much of my mother—sincere, honest, hard working, caring, and very considerate. She made my stay in Vienna a very hospitable one. We talked both in German and English regarding subjects such as religion, politics, economics and societal conventions—always with an open mind. She would ask me some very difficult questions, and I would answer them in German as well as I could. She learned from me, and I learned a lot from her. This made leaving this wonderful flat all the harder. I remember singing "Vien Vien" the day I left, and tears just streamed down her cheeks. I guess I was accepted and was not considered an "Ugly American" whom they had heard about. Believe me, there were a few spoiled brats in our tour group, but I avoided them like the plague. I think wherever I went I changed the attitudes of some regarding their outlook towards the Americans. I felt that this was my obligation as an American, so, as I traveled and met people during that summer, I continued to spread goodwill about America. The third person who I met in Vienna was later to become my wife.

15. Rome/Madrid

The other beautiful and intelligent girl I met later was to become my wife. She was a student at Victoria College at the University of Toronto. My two close friends noticed these three girls with trench coats and cameras while touring the Opera House in Vienna. I didn't have any interest in any girls at that time because of my association with the secretary that I mentioned earlier. They needed a third person because of the number of girls involved and because I knew the city very well. The young ladies were driving their friend's new Volkswagen, and they later would ship it back to Toronto, Canada, as a used car. That was the thing to do in those days. We all crammed into this little Beetle, and off we went for three very lovely evenings. On the third evening we were trying to find a restaurant which I had visited a few times, but I was unable to find it because of the torrential downpour we were having. It was located downtown near the building where they kept the famous white Viennese horses. Finally, we got out of the car and tried to find it on foot, but to no avail. In our conversation, I really felt this girl had all the attributes of a woman I would like to have as a wife. Again I brushed it off because this was no time to get serious; besides we were different culturally, socially, and economically. My thinking at that time would be to marry a Mexican woman who lived in or near California. I could not even think of anything like marriage, especially with this beautiful and petite Canadian. The six of us had a great time especially with the "Beetle" to take us around the places that I had been shown earlier. It was strange, but this young lady and I had seen each other only for three evenings, yet I knew there would be another time. We exchanged addresses and our first correspondence was around Christmas time of 1958.

I continued my courses at the University, and our mid-term break took us to Lublijana and Trieste, Yugoslavia, and Venice, Italy. This was truly an experience but I couldn't keep my mind off the two wonderful people I met in Vienna. The people were similar in

Yugoslavia and in Italy, but I was just a tourist there. I really couldn't get to know the people as I did in Vienna. We returned to classes for a few more weeks and then the summer session came to an end. We had a wonderful first-class dinner the night before most of us were to leave. We were to meet at Southampton, England, a week later but we could go our separate ways at this point. I described the emotional departure from the train station earlier and my plan was to go to Rome by train, fly to Madrid and then on to England. The train trip to Rome was very interesting. I went by coach and sat with four other people. The train clickty clacked down the tracks through Italy. There was a German aboard, along with several Italians. I could communicate with the German, but my Italian was very limited. During the day, I saw much of the landscape and geography. I could understand why the Italian farmers did so well when they came to the United States. They made very good use of every arable acre of land that was available in Italy. I saw double and triple cropping of various types of vegetables and fruit trees. When they had the opportunity to buy a piece of fertile land in California, it was obvious that they were going to get the fullest production from each acre. Like most farmers they had a deep appreciation for the soil and took very good care of it. Much of northern Italy was verdant, but as we got closer to Rome, the landscape became very arid. When I left the train station to make my way to my hotel room, I was amazed and rather bewildered with the traffic and the number of cars in and around the city. I made it to my hotel in one piece, rested, washed, and off I walked to several points of interest. From my hotel I could walk to the statute of Emmanuel III, to the Coliseum, Fountain of Trevei, and finally to the Vatican. The latter had to be the highlight of all the monuments in Rome. There are many, many others which are outstanding but this really impressed me. As I walked down the center of the street leading to the Vatican Basilica, goose pimples ran up and down my arms. I had seen Notre Dame in Paris and St. Stephens in Vienna, but this had to be by far the most impressive of all without taking anything away from the others. I kept saying to myself, is this real—how could a poor boy like me travel so far? I spent three days in Rome and promised I would come back.

Julius C. Manrique, Ed.D.

Little did I know that would never happen because of many complications and circumstances. I left Rome and flew to Madrid, Spain. I wanted to see the country from which my great grandparents came. Most Mexicans have some Spanish blood and culture, and for sure they have the language in them.

It took me a long time to realize that there was a difference between saying I'm "Spanish" when really you were of Mexican descent. As a boy, a close friend of mine always said he was "Spanish" yet his dad and mother both came from Mexico, and he was much darker than I. I couldn't get over this when my father had very light colored skin, almost white, and my mother was a native Californian and yet I always said I was "Mexican." I guess because my father was proud to be from Mexico and he never was ashamed of his heritage. Too many Mexicans say they are Spanish when they are not for various reason—I guess because Spaniards are more acceptable in the United States because they are very light skinned, while typical Mexicans are darker and do menial jobs, working in the fields doing back breaking work that others won't do, and many picture them on welfare with several children. Most Americans really don't realize how much the Mexicans have contributed to the growth and development of this country and, if they do, they will not admit it. Just look throughout the Southwest and in California to see the number of cities with Spanish names. Just look at the number of fruits and vegetables that were cultivated by the Mexicans.

I really don't believe that most Mexican-Americans in the United States want all the territory that was literally stolen from Mexico, returned to them or Mexico, but they want recognition and the opportunity for a better life for them and their children. Most people want to be treated with respect and want to be recognized for their achievements and the Mexican-Americans are no different. The prejudice against the Mexican is deeply instilled in racists' minds and all Mexicans are then stereotyped.

I wanted to see Spain so I could understand my past a little better, knowledge which would help me in the future.

On the airplane I kept staring out the window and trying to take pictures of the landscape below. I was fascinated with each movement of the airplane and the Mediterranean Sea below. Across the aisle was an elderly man, and we struck up a conversation. I found out that he was an American executive whose main base of operation was in Athens, Greece. He was rather important because he got permission for me to sit in the co-pilot's seat and take some pictures from that separate vantage point. Later that night, he arranged a guide for my first night in Madrid. I corresponded with him for sometime until his death a few years later. But from the time I stepped off the airplane and until I boarded again three days later, I used my Spanish language fluently. I remember going dancing the first night, and as I danced, the girls spoke to me and I responded. Never once did they think I was a foreigner or that I was a Mexican-American from California. I had three wonderful days and nights in Madrid. Other than a tour to Toledo, I remained in Madrid and walked and talked to many. I looked for the name Manrique all over—in the telephone books, city hall, etc. I did find the name inscribed in a small church in Toledo. I did not inquire why this had happened. During my studies of Spanish literature, I learned there was a famous poet named Jorge Manrique and, when I took a History of California course, I read that there was a navigator who sailed with Cabrillo named Jaime Manrique. The name comes from Spain like most of the names in Mexico Latin and South America. I also understand that it could have made its way into Spain by way of France and Portugal, but I have not fully traced that those avenues.

Therefore, while touring around the countryside, I saw much resemblance in the territory that reminded me of my state of California. Much of the land was soft and arid, rolling plains just like the land east of my hometown. The living conditions in Spain were very similar to those in Mexico. The white-washed mud adobe huts and homes were almost identical to what I had seen a year ago in many parts of Mexico. I could easily see how much of the Spanish tradition, culture and economics was transplanted to the Americas. I did not find too much about my namesake while in Toledo and Madrid, but I sure learned a lot about geography, the people, how they made their living and why I did certain things as an individual. I knew I could never call myself a Spaniard because of my father's background in Mexico. I would be prouder of the Spanish language and do all I could to perfect the use of it in the future. My days passed quickly and I made my way to the airport for my flight to London, England. As the airplane lifted off the runway and turned northward, I wished that I could come back and spend a little more time studying the country and visiting smaller villages. That would be my hope, but it would be years before that would happen.

16. London/Southampton

Several hours later the airplane approached London and for the first time I was frightened on the landing approach. There was a severe storm and the rain was pelting against the windows. As we descended slower and slower with the wings rocking up and down, a very strange feeling came over me. Maybe this would be it because the pilot was having much difficulty with the airplane in this storm. Finally, the runway and the plane touched the ground safely. I was very much relieved to be on the ground once again. I left the airport immediately for my hotel. All the arrangements were made and I went right to my room to change, shower, and relaxed a little. I arrived a day early so I spent the next day touring London. What an old and grey city I thought as I visited Westminster Abbey, St. Paul's Cathedral, Piccadilly Square, James Park, the British Museum and the Parliament building. I was so exhausted at this point of my tour that when the guide spoke the words went right over my head without any impact.

This was a place that I really wanted to visit again because I really didn't remember too much nor did I read anything much about the places I visited. I guess my mind just couldn't absorb any more. I left the hotel and made my way to the railway station. After a little delay, I boarded a train and was off to Southampton to rejoin the group for our passage home. I think I slept most of the way, but what little I saw I really enjoyed. It was a lovely ride and the countryside was beautiful. The small checkerboard farms were something I read about and now they were in front of me I finally made it to the dock where the SS Arcadia was waiting and then boarded, taking each step up the gangplank very reluctantly. I was going home—would I ever be back? How could this poor Mexican-American teacher ever save enough money to attempt this again? Would people think of me as a boastful and ostentatious individual? Would the constant mentioning to my family of Paris, Bonn, Cologne, Heidelberg, Vienna, Lublijana, Trieste, Venice,

Rome, Madrid, London, Quebec, Montreal, New York, etc. set me apart from my family? How would my friends, young and old, react to me when I mentioned some of these travels taken so young in my life? Would my professional peers in my conservative little hometown be envious, jealous, or would they shun me? Many more questions surfaced as I got to the top step and looked back at the city—what about all those lovely people I met along the way? I knew early in life that man comes by here only one time and when he walks that path he should do nothing that he would regret the rest of his life. Be a friend to everyone you meet because you may or may not ever meet them again was the motto I had, and I practiced this most of my life. I felt good that I was not that "ugly American" and the people whom I met had a little different picture of an American, especially of Mexican descent, by having met me.

I boarded the ship and made my way to my cabin. I was assigned to share a cabin with the same person I shared a room with while in Vienna. We shared many fine experiences, and it was a pleasure to see him again. The voyage back was filled with experiences by everyone, and many tears were shed by various individuals because many of us knew our paths would never cross again. We sang and danced and danced and sang some more. The trip back ended quickly.

Before we knew it, we spotted the shores of Canada at the mouth of the St. Lawrence River. I had heard all kinds of commotion going on about six in the morning, so I dressed and went topside. There was a sight that I'll never forget and I would repeat this experience over and over again to my students. Along the deck were huddled refugees or immigrants from Europe who were coming to Canada on a quota system. I could see their eyes were filled with tears and joy. They were muttering to each other Canada, America, Canada, and America. And a father raised his child into his arms and would repeat —look, "Canada, Canada, Canada!" until the child could repeat the words also. They stood there in the foggy, damp weather for hours looking at their new-found country. All the history that I read regarding quotas and immigrants from Europe, Ellis Island etc. came full circle at that moment. I asked myself many times throughout my life why the Mexican immigrants were often treated so badly and with disrespect, for at this moment, I was seeing a country accepting most appreciatively immigrants from Europe. They provided labor and love for this country once they were settled. (As the Canadian economy expanded, so did the need for immigrants.) I left that scene and had breakfast.

It would be only a few hours and we would be docking at Quebec. We were allowed to leave the ship for several hours and I left everyone to see an area that was vivid history to me. I climbed the mountain that General Wolfe and his army had climbed and surprised General Montcalm on the Plains of Abraham. I relived that moment and walked the area around the fort that overlooked the bend in the St. Lawrence. This was a very strategic position for the French and I could now see why the French wanted to keep it under their command. The turning point for the conquest of this territory lay in winning this position. This was a stunning victory for General Wolfe and I was standing on the same battlefield. This event brought real life to my classes as I reviewed it with them and they could feel my enthusiasm about history. I think much of it rubbed off on some students.

We boarded the ship once again and then sailed on to Montreal. That was a quiet and solemn part of our voyage because there all of us would part forever. We said goodbye many times, kissed and hugged each other, boarded taxis to the railway stations and the airport. I boarded the airplane for my trip to Chicago and then off to San Francisco and Modesto. When the airplane landed in Modesto, I could hardly believe that I made the trip. Over sixteen thousand miles within twelve weeks and memories that would last me a lifetime. No one met me at the airport so I took a taxi to the bus depot and then boarded a small bus to my town of Oakdale. I was greeted by my mother and a few of my brothers. They asked me how was the trip—what could I say—me a world traveler at the age of twenty-six. I tried to be as humble as possible but my enthusiasm for the trip just rolled out. I found it hard to contain myself with all the knowledge and experiences. In two summers I saw more than some of my professional peers would see in a lifetime. I knew that so many people just talked about seeing these cities, but I actually did it early in my career. I did not want to wait until retirement to do this. I told all my friends that they should do the things they want to do as soon as it is possible for them. I was a bachelor and had set certain goals for myself before I met the right girl and settled down. I really didn't want to settle down after my two summers of traveling.

17. The Classroom

My third school year started smoothly and I was back in the classroom a place I really enjoyed and thought I would be in forever. I taught eighth grade social studies which included government, geography, history, etc. I covered the curriculum with enthusiasm and with little difficulty. The various experiences that I had were injected during our conversation at every opportunity. The students loved my class and, as I was later told by my superintendent, "The students were lined up and begging to get into my classes and when the bell rang they had to be actually forced to leave." I had many things in my favor compared to my professional peers on the staff. I think the strongest asset was my enthusiasm and interest in helping make the teaching profession better. How, as one teacher this could be done, I didn't know, but I knew that if I made each hour of the day for the students in my classroom the best they had that day the public relations would filter into the homes and the community. I was, as most beginning teachers, very unselfish with my time and I didn't have all the problems and hang-ups that many of my peers had. I was flexible, demanding, consistent, fair, and positive with the brightest as well as the slowest student. I never talked about the students in the coffee room or discussed the families of the students with anyone. This applied to the upper-class as well as the lower-class students. The wealthier families in this little town really had some problems with their children and somehow put a lot of pressure on the school officials to cover up or hush the wrong deeds when they were done. I treated all students fairly and won their approval and support quickly. I would assign to the average student tasks that other teachers would say would be impossible for them to accomplish. The students would complete them and come back for more. I treated the gifted students with a challenge to be leaders and to use their gift to the fullest. I had ideas coming out my ears for them as well as the child at the bottom of the educational ladder. The slower students were as eager to do a project for me to produce a better classroom environment that increased the students' interest and enthusiasm.

If the teacher is only there because there are no other job opportunities this will show through immediately. I talked to many teachers who have told me they wished they would have been in real estate, farming, or some other such business, but they couldn't do that full time so they taught for supplementary income. This was true because the salaries for teachers have always been low in this city, county and nation. The elementary schools have always been looked down upon in our system of education. For many reasons the teaching profession was looked upon as "if you can't find a good job, then teach." It was looked upon as though anyone could teach. During my many years of teaching, that statement was proved wrong. The natural teacher, in my opinion, is born and does the work easily without great fanfare and recognition. The others have to work at it very hard and many drop out because of low wages, emotional problems, disenchantment, lack of interest or because they shouldn't have been in the teaching profession in the first place. Confucius said, "Once you find a job you love, you will never have to go to work." I loved teaching and I never had to go to work.

18. Philmont

During my third year of teaching, I started to plan my next adventure or goal. I guess having graduated from the fruit and vegetable fields in one generation to earn $4,200. a year in 1959 was just next to being in "hog's heaven." I never had so much money, since when I had earned $3.00 a day pruning peach trees just seven years earlier. Making huge sums of money didn't bother me at that period of my life. I was able to save money with that salary and do many of the things I planned to do. The teaching year was very successful again, and school ended as usual in June.

That summer I did two things. I earned my Woodbadge award in scouting, and I took twenty scouts to the Philmont Scout Ranch in Cimmarron, New Mexico. I forgot to mention that I was a Scoutmaster, and each Thursday was taken up with a meeting, plus at least one weekend a month our troop camped someplace. I was also active at the district level at the same time because I wanted to learn many things about Scouting. My trip to Philmont was a very informative one. Philmont is located in the northeastern part of New Mexico with a total of one hundred and thirty-five thousand acres devoted to Scouting. It was beautifully laid out and given to the Boy Scouts of America by Philips Oil of Tulsa, Oklahoma. All the resources on this land were sold to support the expenses incurred at Philmont, we were told. This had to be one of the nicest settings for young men and adults to receive their training by the Boy Scouts of America.

I remember hiking over sixty miles up and down steep mountains and through thick brush. This was a challenge especially for my back. I was very tired at times but I wanted this experiences more that anything else. I bought a small plaque while I was there which has inscribed on it —I Made It! This hung proudly in my office and when I looked at it, I can truly say I made it in more than one way. We took the train from Riverbank down the San Joaquin

Valley, across the Mojave Desert to Williams, Arizona, and then to the Grand Canyon. This was not the first time I had seen the Grand Canyon but it was the first time I walked around in short scout pants and a white western hat with a red neckerchief. I was truly a sight to be hold, but like most adults who are scouts, you become accustomed to it, and then you start to enjoy the program. The boys had twelve hours of free time and were turned loose with no fewer than four in a group. They had to report to one adult every two hours. The boys were very mature and responsible, and we had no problems at all. This brings up the idea of trusting someone to the fullest until something changes your mind.

Trusting and giving young people the responsibility of watching out for themselves is very important for them to mature. Many times responsibility is given to the individual without any example or training for it and then failure occurs. As a classroom teacher and scoutmaster, we had a lot of discussions about being responsible before they were turned loose.

A coincidence happened in the lobby of the museum at Williams, Arizona. Here I was dressed in my scouting outfit—short pants, neckerchief, etc.—when two young ladies crossed the lobby and I said to myself, I know one of those girls, but from where? Being the shy person that I was, I went up to the young lady and I said "Don't I know you from somewhere?" She really smiled and looked me over and said, "You are mistaken." I took my hat off along with my sunglasses and in unison we said Madrid, Spain. Yes, she was a Jewish girl I met while I was on a tour in Madrid. We had lunch and dinner together one day while I was in Spain and I learned something about another religion. As a scout and a scouter I have always had respect for all religions because there really is, in my opinion, one true god which we all worship—we just have different avenues and approaches. We discussed our European experiences during the past year. She and a friend of hers were driving her brother's new car across the country and stopped here in the Grand Canyon to see the sights. She didn't realize I was involved in the Scouting movement, and I indicated that this was my avocation.

This meeting indicated to me once again how small the world was and that the path that I walked in Europe was a good one because she remembered me well after our short conversation. We toured the various rims of the Canyon, and I could not get over the beauty of this enormous crevice. How was this made? Who put it there? As the day came to an end we bid each other farewell, and we went our separate ways never to meet again. Our train proceeded to Raton Pass, New Mexico, where we left the train for Philmont by bus. I was disappointed with the train ride as compared to the European rail system. The efficiency of the United States' rail system was a long way from catching the efficient European rail system.

We spent ten days at the Philmont Ranch, and we had a glorious experience. I watched young scouts and weak leaders turn into young men and better leaders while I was there. Everyone has weaknesses and strengths, but a good leader capitalizes on the strengths, of an individual and helps the person with his weaknesses. I did this with the individuals on our tour and they really developed. I found out later in life that it is easier to help members outside your family than your own children. Your children react much differently to your advice. I found it easier to help students under my supervision than my own family. Not all parents have problems communicating with their children, but the vast majority of them do.

After our hiking tour we boarded the train to Colorado, Springs, Colorado and the United States Air Force Academy. It was a beautiful train ride with the Rockies on the west and desolate land on the east. We arrived too late to have dinner with the cadets, but we did have a tour of the academy. The following day we went to Denver for our trip home on the California Zephyr. This we understood at the time was the best train ride in the West. The accommodations were not that much better than those on the Santa Fe, but we did have some very scenic and picturesque views, especially through the Feather River Canyon in California. This was a spectacular sight, and I enjoyed it very much. We arrived in Stockton, California, glad but weary. I arrived home very tired, so tanned that my mother barely recognized me.

The day after I got home a friend called me and asked if I wanted to grade peaches for him, but I vowed the first year I began teaching that I would never work in the summer, especially in the peaches. Those days would be reserved for trips, community activities, summer school, and professional growth. My teaching salary was not that large, but my conservative nature with money provided me with the skill to save. I knew very hard times, and I was able to put money away and go without some of the conspicuous consumption items that many of my friends indulged in. I knew I could not have my cake and eat it too. I was living on my income and having a good time in the process. This conservative characteristic really raised havoc in my family because I would be kidded very seriously every weekend or when the family got together that I still had the first dollar I earned. Until this day I save a lot more than I spend because this is my nature, but I don't go without anything I need. I have tried to influence others how important it is to save for that rainy day when no income would be coming in. Since then I had the good fortune not only to save money but also to invest a little for the future.

19. The Civil Rights Lesson

September rolled around again, and I was all charged up to go back to my classroom. Notice that I didn't say, "work", because teaching to me was a profession. I wanted to be an example for the students to emulate. It was not too long after the first few months of school that we were back into the swing of things. I really remembered every class and I should have made some notes of the outstanding things I did to make the classes enjoyable each year, but I didn't. One thing I remembered about my third year was the unit of work about the United States Civil War. I had charts, maps, pictures, speeches, pantomines, etc. for student participation and they really got involved with the 14th, 15th, and 16th amendments and all the civil rights movements during the late and '50s.

One thing I did was to have several panels. There were students who favored the south and those who favored the north, plus some along the Mason Dixon Line and some abolitionist. The students were divided by choice into various functions and then committees were set up with leaders. They all prepared for the panels by researching material on the economic, sociological, political and moral aspect of their positions. It was really something for students at this age level to be this knowledgeable of the political process. We started a debate that went on for a week. Excellent research was presented with good debates, and the respect that was shown to the various students was great. Everything went great and I was the judge and jury and had to decide who had the best presentation. I could not decide because they were all so well prepared. I gave the students the top grades and felt that both groups won—they were satisfied with that decision. Over the weekend I just thought about how successful it was, and I really felt good to be a part of that learning process. The first thing Monday morning the Superintendent called me into his office because the Vice-Principal told him some bad news. What had happened late Friday afternoon went something like this. A few of the students who represented the south brought some syrup and feathers to school to "tar and feather" a few abolitionists and more radical northerners. Little did I realize that, during the week, someone asked me about this act and I explained what happened to these people and forgot all about it. Well a few students just fooling around took a couple of the mavericks into the bathroom and poured some syrup on their faces and clothes and then deposited feathers on those areas that had the syrup. No major damage was done and the parents of the boys did not complain or raise hell with me or the school. The boys involved in this affair all volunteered the information to me, and I found out later they were going to do this in my classroom during the last day of the debate but changed their plans because they knew it would really affect my class and they had a lot of respect for me. Well, the Superintendent asked me what I was teaching in the classroom, and after I got my second wind I explained. He didn't reprimand me, he just congratulated me for creating such enthusiasm for this subject. I was very pleased the way he handled it, and later I called the parents of the boys that were involved. They apologized for the action of their boys and praised me for being such an outstanding teacher. Never before in their lives have their children had so much desire, fun, and interest or learned so much about American democracy and our system of government as this year. They all indicated that if I was in trouble with the Superintendent or the Board of Education over this incident they could come right down and support me. I indicated that I wasn't in any hot water over this and that I certainly appreciated their support. (Today, 2006, it would be an entirely different story).

When I entered the classroom that morning, the students were dead silent. They knew that the Superintendent had called me in for a conference and that they had caused the problem. I could see that many were remorseful and their bowed heads told me a lot more. I went on with the attendance and the daily lesson without mentioning the incident. As a matter of fact, I went on many more days after that before the subject came up during one of our discussions. It had to do with the Ku Klux Klan then and the wild west. Then I bored in on how individuals treated individuals and how many innocent people were hurt and frightened in the process. I used this incident as a learning situation several times during the rest of the semester and the year ended without any further incidents.

I guess the climax of the year was during Public School Week when my room was filled with parents and out of the clear blue sky a parent walked in and with a loud voice said, "So you are the paragon that my child has been talking about all year." He repeated it, and other parents clapped and gave me a round of applause. I was a little embarrassed, but appreciated the comment and the fact that teachers were appreciated. This encouraged me to learn more about my profession and to develop more techniques in order to help the students the following years. The year ended with graduation and many of the graduates apologized profusely for what they had done and told me it was the best year they had ever had. I followed some of those students and several of them became teachers—and a couple became history teachers.

20. The National Jamboree Trip

The plans for my summer of 1960 were twofold. One, I would be an assistant scoutmaster at the National Jamboree, which would be held in Colorado Springs, Colorado and then I planned to fly to Toronto, Canada, to see a friend to whom I had been writing for two years. I was selected by the Yosemite Area Council to be the assistant scoutmaster for the National Jamboree troop from this area. The scoutmaster and the other assistant had been old, experienced hands and had gone several times before because of the "pull" and "social position" in the community. I learned through this experience that it wasn't always the most qualified who got the leadership roles, but rather those who had the "financial influence" and "social status" in the community. This bothered me because there were many worthy and well-qualified leaders in the field who would have liked to participate in these leadership roles, but they knew they wouldn't be selected. I broke the racial barriers with my leadership role in this council and with this Jamboree Troop.

Remember that I had sixteen boys from my troop eligible to go to the Jamboree, and that definitely influenced the selection committee. I was surprised when I was selected because I was prepared for the other response. We got along very well, as good scouters usually do. I was in charge of activities, and did we have plenty to keep the boys busy. We prepared for many competitive events. We learned how to sing as a troop. We sang everywhere we went, and the enthusiasm and morale were very high. The scoutmaster took out his rocking chair and sat, and I did most of the work on that trip. Our trip started with a train ride north to Oregon, Washington, and into British Columbia. I remembered our ferry ride to Vancouver Island because several times I assembled the boys at different parts of the boat and we would serenade the tourists. "Kumbiya" was one of our favorites. Many times we would have to sing an encore and the boys really enjoyed that. From there to Idaho, Wyoming, and then to Colorado Springs, Colorado. We spent seven great days there and everyone had a great time. The highlight of the week was a visit by President Eisenhower who toured the campsite. I didn't go with the whole contingent to see him because I wasn't feeling too well, but his car went right by our camp site on his way back and I got a good look at the old Commander-in-Chief.

I was not too involved in politics, but I was a registered Democrat and always voted the party line. General Eisenhower was a good man but he sure was not prepared to be President. I never realized it until much later in life that almost everything you do or want to do was tied to politics. I found out later on after suffering a personal defeat that politics was very, very important if you wanted to get on the top of your professional career or climb socially. The final campfire was a memorable one. Some fifty thousand scouts lit a candle, and several songs were sung. The campfire was extinguished and we left the campsite in silence. This was quite a week and it came to a close. We made our way back to California by way of Denver, Feather River Canyon to Stockton, California. From there we separated and went our different ways to tell of our many experiences.

21. The Letters

My next event was getting ready to go to Toronto to see this friend I met while studying in Vienna. She was a graduate student at the University of Toronto. We had been corresponding for some two years, sending about one letter a month. As I indicated earlier, here was a bright, beautiful, energetic, and proper young lady who struck me as a wonderful person and who could make someone a very nice wife. Realizing that over three thousand miles separated us, I decided to find out if we had anything in common. The tickets and reservation were all ready and I was anxious for the trip to Canada. When I read my mail upon returning from the 1960 Jamboree, there was one from her. She told me in the letter not to come because it would be impossible for her to receive me. Well, that's all I needed to satisfy my question of interest so I canceled the trip immediately.

I was not too disappointed when I received her last letter. I read it several times then I discarded it. I never kept any letters after I read them thoroughly, but I should have kept that one. I had just returned from a most enjoyable national Scout Jamboree so I needed a rest anyhow. The words of the letter didn't sink in until several weeks later and that was the end of our correspondence. I guess my feelings grew stronger for her after they stopped coming. Maybe I said something to irritate her? Maybe I should have called or done something different. I began to appreciate her beautiful handwriting and the apparent ease of the words that flowed in her letters. It all seemed to be done with such ease and grace that marked her personality.

Our letters were not of a serious nature. They were basically about over professions and the events that were taking place in our lives at that time. I did not write for an explanation, because the tone of her last letter was fairly final. I was not about to take the initiative and ask to continue this correspondence. My male ego and unwarranted pride would prevent me from doing so. Therefore, there was a void in my life until I received a Christmas card from her in December. I returned a card and shortly after the first of the year our letters resumed for another couple of years. Nothing serious until she and her friend decided to go west to see the World's Fair in Seattle.

I had some time on my hands so I enrolled in an extension course through the University of California for advancement on my teaching salary schedule. I have always tried to take professional units to grow in my profession so I continued to study.

22. Professional Leadership

The summer of 1960 passed rapidly and I found myself back to school once again. There were many things that had happened that year which I remembered. The students were great and the school year once again zoomed by. I made my way through the political chairs of our local teaching association and I became President after being Vice-President, Public Relations Chairman, etc. This was really an interesting year and the experiences in that role affected me the rest of my teaching profession. I really learned that whatever you do, someone can find fault with your ideas and that you cannot satisfy everyone. I remember vividly that I was a strong advocate for professional membership—California Teachers Association. There were members of the staff who didn't belong and could care less. I couldn't get over the apathetic and unprofessional attitude of some of my peers. I really couldn't believe that any teacher wouldn't want to support the State organization, let alone the local one. I really found out when I brought up the suggestion that teachers should belong not only to their local, state professional organization but the national one also-I really got the heat from some staff members. They criticized me vehemently and said I was encroaching upon their individual rights. I learned a lot about the teaching "profession" that year and that is only one of two times in my entire teaching career I felt like getting out. (Not because of the students but because of the people who were in the teaching profession.) Statistics and research have shown that most teachers are from lower and middle class backgrounds and have gone into the profession because it was considered a good profession to be in. Some of these people were poorly equipped for this position but their inability to find another job keeps them in the profession. I have seen some very poor teachers who lack the virtues of a model teacher—they are not consistent, sincere, courteous, or even friendly. Many of them are rather insecure and they really shouldn't be in the classroom. I certainly had my eyes opened that year as I traveled around the county. If I thought I was in a poor situation, then other poorer school districts in the county were really suffering. The poorer the school district, the less money they have to pay their teachers, so consequently the better teachers go where the better salaries are— at that time, the junior colleges, high schools and larger cities. My year as President of the Association exposed me to some dedicated and qualified teachers also, so I really followed a philosophy I had established when I went into teaching.

Everybody has problems and everybody is short-suited in some area. The thing to do is not to wail and complain about these, but to do something positive to help solve and overcome them. Avoid focusing in on their weaknesses or their disabilities, rather on their strengths. This principle was one that kept me in the classroom and the profession for more than forty years. At times I became quite irritable with my peers when they would criticize their own profession and when they displayed disinterest in doing the best possible job each day. I learned quickly that there were many factions: one would be the doers; one would just get by; one would be the most critical without any ideas or they being the ones who were passed over for certain jobs or positions. This remained firmly fixed in my mind throughout my profession, and, in my opinion, exists at all levels. I was rather happy the year ended so my term as President was up. There were a few people who wanted me to run again but I declined that honor and I never became active in a leadership role again until I was selected President of Phi Delta Kappa—a professional organization many years later and Chairman of the University of the Pacific Alumni Council.

As President of the Modesto Field Chapter of the Phi Delta Kappa, I tried to provide educational meetings that were informative and interesting. This chapter had its good days, but it slowly declined in membership and I believe went out of business. Most of the members were only interested in a social atmosphere and cared little about an educational meeting.

My experience as Chairman of the University of the Pacific Education Alumni Council was a very challenging one. When I was asked to chair the council I proposed certain conditions to the Dean of the School of Education. He accepted and I changed the council from the "Good Old Boy" council to a widely diverse group that included at least 50% women. We really accomplished a lot in the few years that I was on this council by enlarging the council to include a diverse group of educators. The council had subcommittees that reported at each meeting with certain objectives to be accomplished during the year. As chairman of the council provided me with a very enriching experience.

23. Catching My Breath

During the summer of 1961, I enrolled at San Jose State University to prepare for my Masters Degree. I took both the six and four week session in order to progress as rapidly as possible. The courses were very interesting, and I was quite happy back in the classroom under different circumstances. I had a job, a little security, traveled to Europe, and done a lot of things many people in the classroom hadn't done. I was ready to complete my next goal—the Masters. I kept telling myself, "Si, se puede." It was an important step for me because without the Masters I would remain at the same pay level forever.

Many of my professional peers worked in the peaches during the summer months and made a few extra dollars, but I remained true to my vow. They always said it was a change of pace; it helped them relax; they met people of different social classes; and they really understood them and their children better. All of these were pretenses in my opinion. It just proved to me that they didn't think enough of the teaching profession to improve their skills and knowledge, and it displayed to the public that they only worked nine months out the year and they worked during the summer to make additional money. Why should the public pay them anymore? This attitude prevailed throughout our area and really got very bad years later. The summer slipped by quickly, and I was very pleased with the progress I made toward my Masters. A couple of more summers like this one and I would have my goal accomplished. I had the enthusiasm necessary to do a good job. Remembering great works are often performed not by strength but perseverance. I had several goals and I would aim for them. Life is drab and meaningless to those who do not set certain goals and commit themselves to seeking them. Wise people learn to make their own fortunes. They give themselves heart and soul to do something beyond the satisfaction of today's wants. They consider the ways in which to determine their own future right now. The time at school was necessary for me because it was a pause, a change, a

Julius C. Manrique, Ed.D.

break in my career, and it gave me the time necessary to understand myself, assess current happenings and weigh my progress toward the attainment of my long-term expectations.

24. Community Service Dampened

I was back in school the fall of 1961, and two things happened that year that altered my personal and community goals. The most severe one I'll explain first. It is necessary to have suffered first before you can find happiness. When suffering comes, it is necessary to have the fortitude to weather the storm. The first had to do with my scouting activities. As was mentioned earlier, I was a scoutmaster and we had a thriving troop. It was about fifty in number, and many times we had to meet outside the community center. It was at that time when I was a few minutes late to my usual time of 6:45 p.m.; (troop meeting starting time was 7 p.m.) and two scouts were fighting over a golf club that had nothing to do with the meeting. They were playing with the golf clubs of a friend across from the community center and arguing about whose turn it was to swing the golf club. One of the boys was swinging the golf club, and the other boy walked into the swing and the golf club hit him on the temple. He fell to the ground and lay very still. I just pulled up at the meeting place when this had happened. The scout rushed over to me and told me what had happened. I rushed in for the first aid kit, and I was on my way to help the boy. The scouts all acted as they were trained and no one panicked. The golf club opened up a gash about four inches on the side of the boys' head. I applied some bandages around the head and carried him to my car. I then rushed him to the local hospital for further care. He was placed in the emergency ward for immediate care. After some wait, the doctor completed the necessary stitches, and he was ready to release him when I asked the doctor, "How are the X-rays?" He said, "We didn't take any and it didn't look necessary." I said, I wouldn't leave there without him having X-rays. After a little disagreement, the doctor in charge reluctantly ordered X-rays of the head. The X-rays showed a small bone lodged against the brain, and it should have been removed immediately. The Oakdale Hospital at that time did not have the equipment so the scout was rushed to the St. Joseph's hospital in

Stockton, 30 miles away. That evening a successful operation was performed, but the young man was extremely overweight and other complications began to occur. He was placed on the critical list for several days, which seemed like eternity.

I had the entire troop covered with insurance, but the insurance company refused to cover this accident because of a minor technicality. It happened before the meeting started and not in the vicinity of the meeting place. I argued strongly that they should honor the policy, but the local office refused to pay the medical expenses incurred by the scout. I finally talked to several members of the local Lions Club about this because I was really sick about the accident and concerned about the scout's medical care and expenses. The family couldn't afford the hospital costs. Finally, after a little pressure from different influential sources, the insurance company came through, and the costs were taken care of. After three days on the critical list, he was taken off and remained in the hospital several more weeks. He was released to go home, but he couldn't participate in any activities for quite some time. Wherever he went, he wore a helmet for protection. Several months later, he was released to return to school and many of his peers treated him royally, and others who didn't know what had happened, treated him poorly. He had problems with his vision and he had black spots appearing every once in awhile. The doctors said that was normal for such a blow and he should grow out of it. Many years later I met him and this was true with the exception of the dark spots occurring from time to time.

This accident really made me think about all the responsibilities I had which I didn't realize. My enthusiasm for a direct leadership for scouting dampened considerably and I requested the troop committee to look for a replacement because I was stepping down the following June. The committee didn't look too hard because I had two fine assistants, but both of them declined to take over. This search went on all summer, but there was no replacement. I asked an old school friend of mine who was a former Eagle Scout if he would be interested, and he accepted. I told the committee, and they accepted my resignation. I felt sick about this, but that accident really had an affect on me and my scouting career. I learned so much about people, the system, the scouting movement, people in the insurance companies and their philosophy, doctors and some parents. I decided to do something for myself for a change and just enjoy my simple life.

That year, I was honored by the local Parent Teachers Association as their choice for honorary life membership as a worthy individual in the community. I didn't realize this was to happen, but after I got the award, I guess I knew the "right people." This is how most outstanding awards or plaques are awarded. You have to know someone on the nominating committee, and if you made someone on that committee angry, good luck! This I found out was prevalent in most organizations, and it was something that was acceptable. I even know of one individual who never got any awards so he started his own organization and had the nominating committee give him the first award. From that point, he would make sure he was in line for awards that he placed upon his office wall. It is not what you know or what you have done, but it is whom you know that counts in this country. I couldn't believe that this change of attitude was happening to me, but I just had to get away from the scouting movement for awhile. I really wanted one of my two assistants to take over the troop, but both gave the excuse they were too busy—that I could understand. I could accept that from one of them because he had very little experience in scouting, but the other one had the ideal situation to be the next leader. I tried to help a friend of mine who took over the troop, but either you have it or you don't. He didn't have the leadership ability that we thought he had and the troop immediately floundered. He hung on, and the troop went down hill for several years until he gave up, and another leader step in.

It is a shame that parents who could easily take over leadership roles in the community rarely step forward because they would rather have someone else do all the work so their children can enjoy these activities. Many of them have good reasons, but through experience I found out that many of them just didn't want to work or

103

be bothered with someone else's children. This rang loud and clear when I tried to find a leader for this troop.

I stepped down and out of a leadership role. I left the troop but became the Troop Chairman for several years. This gave me the opportunity to become a little active in the Lions Club, a local service organization. It didn't take me long to go through the chairs. I started as a director and then third vice president. I attended many meetings and then finally withdrew my membership because I felt these kinds of organizations were not for me. I was not a joiner.

I found out later in life when I ran for an elective office that one had to cultivate members of these and other service clubs or your chance for election to an office is very small. In my opinion, I feel the people who join these organizations are in need of strokes, are egotistical and have a great need for attention. Some of their antics are so juvenile it is hard to believe. I read somewhere that Americans are so self-conscious about the need to belong to groups that they have the highest number of memberships in all kinds of groups, be they service, social, religious, recreational—they just have to belong to something or they feel left out. I left the Lions Club and the Scoutmaster role within a period of two years. I continued working at the district level for many more years, but even that became so political that I withdrew from many of those activities.

25. The Engagement

During the 1961-62 school year things went along very normally, and I planned to attend summer school during the summer of 1962. I was looking forward to attending school at San Jose State University and continuing work on my Masters Degree. It was during the school year that my friend from Toronto, Canada, decided to come to see the World's Fair which was located in Seattle, Washington. I invited her to California and I would show her a few sites if she were interested. A letter came from Toronto indicating that she was bringing a friend and that she was traveling in her little Vauxhall (British-made car). It was a jewel of a car and tremendous on gasoline—thirty-five miles to a gallon for a 1960 car. The school year ended, and I enrolled in summer school. I had a close friend who lived in Sunnyvale, and we made arrangements for him to meet with her friend. She and her friend made their way across the northern part of the United States to Seattle. There they stayed for several days and then came down the coast to San Francisco. She called me from San Francisco during the middle of the week, and I went to the city to meet them. I took them both to dinner and showed them a few sights of San Francisco by myself because my friend was busy that night. It was as though I had known her for some time because our conversation began from where it left off years ago. I guess this is how it is when you develop a good friendship in life.

I read somewhere that a person is lucky if he develops one or two close friends in a lifetime. During my life time, I have not been able to trust many people because it seemed that someone always wanted something from me, but when I asked for a favor they were hard to come by. She had all the qualities and characteristics I wanted in a wife, i.e., empathy, understanding, unselfishness, hard worker, frugal, conscientious, intelligent, self disciplined, level headed, and beautiful both physically and in her soul. The latter was truly displayed during our marriage by giving of herself to further my education and the rearing of our two daughters. Also it was displayed with her leadership as President of AAUW, Chairperson of the Human Right Commission, Girl Scout Leader, etc.

It was her tenure as chairperson of the Human Rights Commission that her true spirit and soul came out. She had served on this commission for several years and was then asked by the Mayor to be chairperson. She accepted and truly wanted to do an excellent job. This was a window dressing commission and not much was ever done. She proposed many ideas, but they were turned down, and she became frustrated by the inaction of such a worthwhile committee. She defended a black person who was dismissed from a city job which caused repercussions at City Hall. She had differences with the Mayor and later resigned. Many of her ideas were used by the succeeding chairperson.

My friend and I decided to take them to Monterey that weekend. It was a beautiful day to drive to the coast. Our discussions moved from one item to another, and we felt like tour guides. It was at Monterey that our feeling between us finally came out into the open. I really loved this girl, but I resisted showing it because of the distance between her home and California. It was not fair for her to leave all of her friends and family to settle here in California. The climax of the day was when we were having dinner on the wharf. She couldn't eat a thing for dinner but sometime before or later, I don't recall, I asked for her hand in marriage. She accepted and the next few days were glorious for both of us.

I just wished that the miles between us had been shorter, because our engagement period was very short. I took her to my home to meet a few of my friends and my mother. Naturally, my mother was elated. You see, I was the last of nine boys to marry. I was thirty years old and she thought I would remain a bachelor forever. This is quite characteristic of people of her generation to want to have their children settle down. She and my friend hit it off immediately. There wasn't a person that my mother didn't like, and, until the time of her death, she never disliked anyone—she was truly amazing.

She and I traveled through the various parts of the valley, but just being together after four years was enough. It is strange that, when people are in love, they don't have to say a word to communicate. Your eyes, hands, and body movements while walking all communicate a love and desire for each other. If only that feeling could be maintained at all times, marriages would last forever and ever. Failing to communicate seems to be the destruction of so many marriages, and somehow it is this ability that God has given us but we fail to use it during the rough times of marriages. She was readily accepted by all of my acquaintances. It is strange that in our country we develop many acquaintances, but we have very few close friends. I was to find this out later in my life. The time which she allotted on her vacation had come to a close and she had to make her way back to Toronto. She and her friend left for their long journey home in their little Vauxhall. I would write to her in about a week and then send a letter to her father and mother formally asking permission to be married. I had a strange feeling about this, but I wanted to, so I wrote and asked for permission. Her father wrote back and gave us permission with only one request. It was the most difficult thing for me to do during our marriage especially when there were difficult times and many strong disagreements between two very strong personalities. He requested that I always try to make her "happy." I indicated that I would try to carry out this wish, but as the years flew by there were times that I didn't, for one reason or the another.

I then made arrangements to fly to Toronto during the Christmas holidays of 1962. Arrangements were made, and my friend decided to go with me.

The school year started the same as usual without any hitches or problems. I loved my job and really didn't mind what my peers and administrators were up to. It is hard to believe now after all these years that an administrative position was never offered to me while I was teaching in Oakdale. It took me years to find out that a person had to be aggressive in order to gain recognition for some of these positions and then it had to be at the right time and you had to know the right people above you. I also found out that if you were aggressive at the wrong time you were labeled a rabble-rouser, radical, a tiger, Red, Communist, liberal, etc. by the powers that be.

Many of these leaders of the community who are in power want yes men or women so they can control them. They really don't want thinkers. When one offers a suggestion that will change something, you are laughed at and the suggestion is discarded. But when the right person makes the changes, then that person gets the credit and recognition for that great idea. Thank goodness I didn't know this during my formative teaching years or I would have changed professions during the first few years. I found out that I really couldn't recommend anyone into the profession after I had over twenty years of service. There were just too many hypocrites in the teaching profession and I guess in some respects I became one of them also. I could not get out of the profession after twenty years of service and the number of years of education. I had to just float along until something else came along.

The Christmas holidays of 1962 were beautiful. After a fog-delayed flight from San Francisco to Toronto, we arrived a day late. Little did I know that my friend had planned an engagement party and invited her very close friends. There was quite a houseful that evening. When she met me at the airport I knew I had made the right choice and I hoped that her parents would accept me as their future son-in-law. I was quite apprehensive when we drove up the driveway, and they greeted me at the door. I'll always remember that day because it taught me to always be myself and everything will work out. Her father was very relaxed, and we hit it off very easily. He was a man in his early sixties, and he worked in the personnel office at the headquarters of Imperial Oil Company. He was about ready to retire, and the company did have plans to retire many of the people in his age bracket. My future mother-in-law seemed to be a little reluctant to accept me at first, but it didn't take long for me to relieve her apprehension that she had about me. My friend had two sisters, one sixteen months younger, one eight years younger than she. The second daughter was already married to a young executive who worked for the Imperial Oil Company. (He later took over as a service station manager because he wanted to work for himself—he did quite well.) There seemed to be a little competition between the two but I never mentioned it until my friend and I discussed it many years later. We got along very well and there never seemed to be any friction other than she always had to have something a little better or has taken a trip here or there before we had. The party was very successful and I really talked that night, answering questions about California. The two weeks just zoomed by and I had to leave Toronto and return home to California. Something happened on the way to the airport that has reoccurred throughout my life and caused many headaches for her. I became quite silent and my friend asked me several times if anything was wrong. It was strange, the more she asked me the quieter I became. Had I made a mistake? Had she picked the wrong person? I kissed her farewell and boarded the airplane and seated myself near a window.

The airplane took off and I was on my way home. I kept saying—did I make the right choice? Is this the right thing to do? How can I make her happy so far away from her friends? Am I the right choice for her? All of these questions went through my mind. I was happy but yet sad. How could this be happening to me? A graduate from the fruit fields about to marry this very lovely, beautiful, and intelligent woman from a large city of Toronto. We had no language barriers. We had no educational barriers, but our socio-cultural differences would bother me all my life, even though she never mentioned it until late into our marriage.

It is fortunate when two people marry within the same socio-economic and cultural background, but that doesn't happen too often now in the United States with the great number of interracial marriages. Democracy has permitted almost everyone a free choice and the opportunity to enjoy the fruits of one's labor. Maybe this is good because it brings out the best genes that both individuals can produce. This makes up much of the middle class society who really work at being good citizens. When the airplane landed in San Francisco, I immediately got off the plane and ran to the nearest telephone. I called her at 9 p.m. West Coast time. I just had to tell her that I made the right decision and that I hoped she did also. She did say yes and the burden was lifted off my shoulders. I left the airport to pick up my car in

Sunnyvale. I had one very difficult time getting there, but after several hours I finally picked up my car and I was on my way home in the wee hours of the morning. The drive to Oakdale took about two and half hours, and I arrived home about the time the sun was coming up. My mother thought I would never make it, because I had to work the next day. I took a shower, had breakfast, and went off to work with just a catnap. That was really a fantastic Christmas holiday, and I would remember it the rest of my life.

26. Annual Eagle Scout Recognition Dinners

I didn't realize that I was to be honored by the Yosemite Area Council as one of the outstanding scouters of the year on her birthday, January 19, 1963. I received the highest award the Boy Scouts of America bestows upon an adult scouter in the council—Silver Beaver. I was completely surprised because these awards are usually given to wealthy and prominent executive board members, and I was neither. I guess times were changing and more and more of the scouters who were directly involved with the boys were receiving them. Receiving this award was one of my lifelong dreams as a leader in the council and, in doing so, I would encourage other scoutmasters to do an outstanding job with their boys so they in turn could be recognized. Little did I know, I would be recognized at the age of thirty for this leadership role. What would be my next goal in Scouting? The Silver Antelope, Silver Buffalo? No these were way out of my reach because of social and economic positions in life. I knew full well how these individuals were selected for these. I feel it is wrong, but how else could the movement exist without these recipients giving so much financial leadership to this organization? This is one fact of life I learned very early in my scouting career and I did not think about receiving any further Scouting awards.

I may be wrong, but I don't think anyone of Mexican descent has ever received any of these Regional or National Awards (when I was in Scouting). This can be attributed to the lack of interest by many Mexicans in the Boy Scouts. They lack the desire to get extremely involved in the program. I was a little different, and when the new executive asked me to be on the executive board, I said yes on one condition—that he wouldn't put artificial barriers in my way if I had some ideas for change. I was appointed Vice President of the Advancement for the Council because of my interest and experience in that area. This was my first love and I set out to make the council

111

an outstanding one. So it didn't take me long to develop a cadre of scouters who worked as hard as I did to really make advancement the corner stone of scouting for the council. We developed policy, format for courts of honors, advancement teams, and district.

We had more than seventy-five Eagles at the first annual recognition dinner, all sponsored by an adult in the profession of their choice. For seven years we had these recognition dinners and our Boy Scout advancement just skyrocketed. The highlight of my scouting career in this position was the opportunity to be M.C. and to introduce Mr. James Stewart at one of the Annual Eagle Scout Recognition Dinners. I was rather apprehensive all day and when I met him at the airport and shook his hand all the apprehension was gone. Here was a kind and gentle individual who was giving his time to help this movement. Our dinner was held at the officers' club at Castle Air Base, Merced, California. The room was jam packed, and there was standing room only. I took care of all the formalities; then I introduced Jimmy Stewart. I thought for a moment—is this really me doing this! I took my time introducing him and when I finished he said "that was a real nice, fine introduction. I've never been introduced that way before." I said thank you, and he delivered his speech. His speech was prepared with all the pauses typed—I could see his written speech from where I was sitting.

If we could only open our eyes and learn from each other without biases, hatred, and jealousies getting in our way, what a great world this would be. I learned much from this two-hour meeting with this outstanding gentleman. After the speech he remained another hour or so autographing his picture on the programs that were available. I realized that God has given each of us some ability and the only thing we have to do in life is to find our strengths and develop them as Mr. Stewart has done. The only thing wrong with that is many of us take a lifetime to find our strengths and then it is too late in life to make any contributions. Another thing wrong with that "adage" is that many times it is whom you know and not what you know that gives you the breaks in life.

27. 4-H Camp Director

During the summer of 1963, I had the opportunity to be camp director for the 4-H group in Stanislaus County. This was rather unusual for me since it was a mixed group of boys and girls. I had worked at scout camps, but this proved to be very interesting. The program was well planned and the camp opened up without any hitches. It was located near Lake Pinecrest and a small resort area, which made it an ideal location. The 4-H'ers were just a great group of young boys and girls. The only crisis I had was on the Saturday night before closing. We were going to have their annual dance and several non-4-H'ers were going to crash the dance. I told the young leaders (counselors) that if they did crash the dance I would stop the dance and recommend to the County Advisor not to have the dance again.

The dance went on, and I was told who the intruders were. I asked them very politely to step outside with me for a short discussion. I could tell by the way they walked and talked that they were under the influence of alcohol. The four young men followed me out of the hall and down the road towards the resort. We talked and talked and talked in a very rational manner. I realized they were looking for something to do and to have some fun. At any time the four of them could have easily pounced on me and taken off, but I think I was reasonable, cool, calm, and collected with them, and they sensed it. I treated them with respect, and they realized it. I learned that all people want to be treated with courtesy and when you appeal to their reasoning power, they will usually abide by a joint decision. The boys decided to leave without any trouble and they shook my hand in the process.

I felt I had matured several years to have handled those young men in that manner. The events could have easily gone the other way and it could have been very messy. It was important to the

Julius C. Manrique, Ed.D.

camp staff and to me that this annual event continue. I think we both succeeded because the board asked me back the following year.

28. The Wedding Day/Honeymoon

The summer of l963 was important for me for another reason. On July 20, l963, we were married in the Leaside United Church of Canada. I remember the day very clearly because during the ceremony thunder and lightening cracked very loudly and there was an eclipse of the sun and the day grew very dark. I wonder if the Lord was telling us something. Also, when the minister asked her if she would accept me as her husband, she lost her voice and uttered I do. I did not know it at the time, but the young lady who was to sing for us also got sick the night before, and she was unable to sing so we just had music instead.

After the ceremony, we drove to the reception at the Casa Loma (a beautifully restored castle) in a limousine—my first and only time. It was quite an unusual feeling for the poor boy from the East Side of the tracks to be experiencing this upper-class event. Pictures and the congratulation line were in order when we arrived at the Castle. This took several hours and then the reception, which included a buffet dinner. The sky grew black, and it became very dark outside because of the eclipse of the sun that was mentioned earlier. This happened just before the toast was given by the best man and a very close friend of the family. I don't quite remember what my brother-in-law said, but I remember vividly what the close friend of the family said. He went on describing how he knew the family and ended by saying that this marriage would bring together the Spanish blood with the Scottish.

I did not know how to take that comment with this very friendly group, but I thought about that for years and years after that. I took it in a positive way because it tends to bring out the best from both individuals. I accepted the toast and then gave a little speech. I don't remember what I said, but I did praise the institution of marriage and described it as a rudder in life. I asked the group to imagine a leaf floating down a small stream into a larger one.

How it floated all over without any sense of direction similar to an individual who floats along through life without any major sense of direction until he or she meets someone they wish to spend their life with and marry. The institution of marriage gives the couple a sense of direction with many goals to aim for during their lives together. The marriage performs as a rudder in one's life and an individual sets out to help the other partner as they move through different stages of their life. I felt pretty relaxed after my little speech and then my wife and I passed out small pieces of wedding cake, which was made by my mother-in-law. This was a custom they had and it gave the wedding couple a chance to meet the guests personally and thank them for coming.

My life was entering into another phase that would help me find some of my strengths and weaknesses. The afternoon came to a close and we departed in her little Vauxhall for our honeymoon in Quebec. We spent the first night at the Inn on the Park, a beautiful hotel north of the city. The next day we floated out of the city going north to Quebec. We drove no more that two hundred miles a day. The first stop was in Kingston where we visited an old battlefield where the Canadians defeated the Americans during the War of 1812-1814. We met a close family friend there strolling through the grounds. They were very close friends of the family, and I remembered them very well. During my first visit to my in-laws home, I was in one corner of the room with her friends asking me all kinds of questions about California, and he noticed this and rescued me from the crowd by taking me into the kitchen. That was really a relief, and I never forgot him for the fine goodwill gesture. Well, we had a good chat with them and then left for Montreal.

While in Montreal we met other friends of my wife and had dinner with them. This was a young couple that went through school with my wife and were very close school friends. We made arrangements to stay at the Holiday Inn in Quebec and during the evening we ran across my friend who was on his honeymoon also. He informed me that they got married the exact time and date that we did. That was the reason he did not attend our wedding. This was a little disappointing, but we accepted it. We became very close friends while living in California. He did something that I should have done, but I never gave it serious thought. After living in Sunnyvale for five years, he was laid off his job at Lockheed. His wife wanted to move back to Toronto to be close to her family. Since he didn't have a job. They sold their home and moved.

It was something I should have seriously considered so my wife could be close to her friends and relatives, but it never occurred to me until it was too late in our marriage and our daughters were much older by then. I think that would have helped our marriage if I had done that and would have fulfilled my father-in-law's request to make her happier. We toured the city of Quebec for several days and then placed the car on a steamboat and sailed out the St. Lawrence and up the Saganay River to Chicoutimi where we spent the night in a lovely motel. From there we drove down through the Laurentians. This part of the country was beautiful, but I guess the desert would have been beautiful in our situation.

Why doesn't this feeling for each other last longer? Why does it end so soon in one's life? The expression "it is better to have loved and lost, than to have never loved at all" has to be a classic one because I am sure every newlywed has experienced this feeling. I guess if you analyze one's marriage, you would find that if the foundation or love is strongly built, the marriage will last. We made our way back to Toronto to see the family for the last time that year. We loaded up the Vauxhall with all of our wedding presents and we left for California.

We took the northern route back. Our first stop was Lansing, Michigan. Then we moved north through the great Mesabi Range. As a history teacher, I had talked about this area and I really wanted to visit it very much. This huge open pit was mind boggling. I had never seen such a huge man-made hole. Then we moved west through Minnesota and the Dakotas to see the Black Hills and the carved figures of our four great presidents on Mount Rushmore. The magnitude of these carvings was hard to comprehend. We then traveled to Yellowstone National Park—what beautiful scenery. The geysers were as beautiful and picturesque just as they were described in the books. Then we drove through Montana to see the huge copper fields and smelting plants of the Anaconda Copper Company. From there to Spokane, Washington, and the Great Grand Coulee Dam. I had seen the Hoover Dam which is the highest concrete dam in the world, but the Grand Coulee was the widest dam in the world up to that time. It was immense! It was gigantic! We could hardly believe our eyes when we took a tour of it. We were overwhelmed by this huge structure. Dams have always impressed me and this was the ultimate—no other dam would ever impress me again even though California has an exceptional irrigation system that is the envy of the world.

We left this area and headed south through Oregon and to beautiful Crater Lake. This is a remarkable lake with its crystal clear water. We left there to enter northern California and finally to Modesto where we lived a few days before finding an apartment. The trip took us fifteen days and my wife's faithful Vauxhall made it all the way with no problems. It averaged about thirty miles to a gallon with little use of oil, other than the changes. We kept this little car until late 1973 when we reluctantly sold it to a neighbor. We would still see the car from time to time parked in a vineyard as a decoy to give people the impression someone was at this farm.

29. My Wife

My sister Alice had planned a reception for us at the end of August and about two hundred people attended. It was a pleasure to see so many acquaintances that I had gotten to know during the last few years. A few of them thought I would never get married so they showed up to kid me a little. All of them were favorably impressed with my choice and told me many times later that my wife was a first-class person. There was no doubt in my mind that my wife was a very fine person and she displayed it in later years. The reception was beautiful and the day ended quickly.

We spent several days at my mother's home (the house I was born in) and immediately my wife was in for a cultural shock. Many of the meals and the manner in which they were prepared were not like they were prepared in her home. I could see her reaction and I asked her to tolerate it for a day or so until our apartment was ready. After a few days we moved into our own apartment in Modesto because that is where my wife was appointed to a teaching job. I would commute to Oakdale until I found a job in Modesto.

My wife would always love my mother until the time of her death—they got along very well and my mother would tell me over and over again how nice my wife was. My mother always had a good word for my wife when I visited Oakdale by myself. Our family life started in Modesto in September of 1963. We moved into a semi-furnished apartment until we could buy a few things. During our marriage, we never purchased anything on time with the exception of our home. We never purchased anything beyond our buying power. If we saw something we wanted, we would save for it and pay cash for it. Our saving habits were the same. Due to our backgrounds, we had different reasons for saving. In my case it was always being in the state of poverty and never knowing where your next meal was coming from that made me save and save. My wife saved because it was part of the Scottish heritage. It was a natural thing for her to do and it was part of their culture.

The first purchase for our marriage was a dinette set. We purchased it on sale and received a free twenty-pound turkey with it. We had that set for almost a lifetime. It really held up beautifully, and it displayed how we took care of items that we purchased. We still have our original electric lawn mower that is over thirty-six years old and still cutting very well. We then proceeded to buy some major pieces of furniture, but it was always with the idea we would pay cash for it. My wife was teaching at one of the local high schools and I was still teaching in Oakdale sixteen miles away. She had a very beautiful educational background and was an expert in teaching English, French and could teach German and Latin if necessary.

She could have easily been a lawyer or doctor if she had been encouraged by her professors to enter one of those fields, but she always wanted to be a teacher partly because her parents approved and it was the thing to do for her social and economic class. It was a step up the social and economic ladder from her parent's educational and social level. Later in life, she would question that decision and spend many trying months deciding what to do with her life especially after the children were in school and left the nest. She was a classic example of a very bright woman never being encouraged by male professors to enter into a different profession other than teaching. She did, by the way, enter into a Doctoral program while teaching at the university level, but became an A.B.D. (all but dissertation) candidate. She enjoyed the experience of a doctoral program, but had no regrets in not finishing the program. She became a full-time non-tenure track teacher at California State University – Stanislaus in Turlock, California, and thoroughly enjoyed teaching at that level. In my opinion she should have started her teaching career at the University level since she was extremely well trained and had the intelligence and skill to compete with anyone in her field. Yes, the glass ceiling kept her from reaching the top also.

30. University Politics

I entered graduate school at the age of forty and immediately ran into that strange feeling—politics at this level also! Boy, did I find out how bad it really was when I challenged a curriculum professor. He was about to retire, but the influence he had on the other staff was unbelievable. You didn't question any professors at the graduate level because they knew it all, and you were suppose to listen and accept their knowledge. This was not true in every class or with every professor, but it was sure true with this one. I discovered that one secures a higher position professionally by not rocking the boat, but by getting to know the "right people." I saw how unfair some districts were with their employees and how good they were to others. For example, all the doctoral students were to be officially full-time and were to be limited in the number of hours they worked in their districts. Several candidates worked full-time and carried a full academic load at the university. That's all right if there wasn't a rule against it. Where were the professional ethics? Another district didn't give one dollar for a sabbatical while another district gave their high school principal full salary while he was away at graduate school. The following year he was appointed assistant superintendent of that same school district.

Where was the fairness? Was there sex discrimination? Yes. One community college English instructor was denied admission into the graduate school after she took a sabbatical, rented an apartment, and enrolled in school. She was given verbal approval over the phone to enroll, but when the graduate committee met, she was denied admission.

Our group of ten doctoral students met at this woman's apartment who was denied admission, for lunch every Thursday to review, plot, plan strategy, collect notes, discuss current problems, prepare for the quals, and just to have a moral support group. Each would be responsible for the main meal and the others would bring whatever they wanted. It was a tremendous thing for me to look forward to each week. We analyzed each of the past questions and test ourselves on the qualifying examination which we were all to take that coming summer. We analyzed the professors and took notes on each of them. We noted their favorite authors and their strange idiosyncrasies. We studied them very hard, and each of us reported to the group every week the items their professors stressed for the week. We obtained copies of their lecture notes (some over ten years old) and we would quiz ourselves on them. Our goal was to have one hundred percent of us who took the quals pass the first time. We were strong morale builders for each other and as the year ended I had five binders filled with specific information that would be answers to the quals. The sessions went by rapidly and I really got to know some current educational material and how to find anything you wanted at the library.

I became acquainted with a couple of professors very well. A professor of education and in charge of research had to be my favorite. I guess because statistics was very difficult and I went to him more than anyone else. When this happens you get to know someone's strengths and weaknesses. He recognized mine and encouraged me to forget about the weaknesses and concentrate on my strengths. He was a great inspiration and friend all through my doctoral program even after he moved to the University of Southern California. I finished the year with over thirty-six units of A's and only two B's in the whole program of forty-eight units. I think it had to do with this professor. Some people are turned off on education early in life and it takes a circumstance or someone to make you realize that God has given you some ability and that you can achieve in spite of those earlier experiences. Why do teachers let this happen to our young and potential resources? Why are we so inhumane with our fellow man? Why does the color of one's skin make a difference who gets the best job or gets ahead? Why are some people given more recognition than others? I had a lot more questions after my doctoral program than when I started.

During my doctoral graduate interviewing process I was asked many questions, but one that I remember vividly was the one regarding my graduate record scores. The Dean of Graduate Studies questioned my scores saying it was just above the average and wondered how I could explain it. The only explanation that I had was that there were a lot of questions on that test I never heard of or ever experienced. I felt that the Graduate Level Examination was culturally biased and that my educational background gave me little exposure to many of these items. I also reminded him that my Miller Analogy scores were much higher than the average and this displayed another kind of intelligence. I answered both of these questions as calmly as possible, but I must have shown some irritation with these technical issues to ease out or prevent culturally-deprived students from entering graduate studies at different levels or professions. I was excused for a few minutes from the interview while they decided my future (a flash back to my fourth and fifth grade decision by those two teachers and the principal) and then was called in again. The chairman made a comment which I never have forgotten. He said, "I think we are fortunate to have Mr. Manrique here at our school and regardless of his age, he will succeed in this program because of his desire to achieve professionally and for his nationality. I know the situation that he is in because I am 'Oriental". That ended the meeting, and a few weeks later I received a letter congratulating me upon successful completion of the preliminary conference. I could now plan for the qualifying examinations and my doctoral dissertation. I signed up for the summer qualification examination, and I felt I was prepared.

You are on your own when you cross that bridge. The summer approached and I prepared for these exams like I never did before. I wanted to be one of the ten to pass them the first time around. It was rather fortunate that my wife was attending a conference for the A.A.U.W. in Washington, D.C., that summer. She took the children to Toronto the summer of 1973 while I prepared and took the examinations. My wife was very active in community affairs and went to great lengths to do the best at all times. She was a dedicated person and always did everything to perfection. She was very helpful to me because I did things very well sometimes, but not to the perfection of my wife. Well, we had one goal the summer of 1973 and that was to pass these quals. I took the major quals the Saturday after she left. That gave me a week to study without the family around. It was an eight hour written examination—Four hours in the morning and four hours in the afternoon. The afternoon test was allowed to go a little longer than four hours. I felt very good after the test because I was well prepared. I never had that experience before, but I wrote like I've never written before. Our group all had dinner together that night and all of us felt very good about the preparation for these tests. We all left to prepare for our second four-hour test that we were allowed to take only if we passed the major qual. A week later I was informed that I had passed and I could proceed to the next one.

The curriculum qual was the next one and I prepared for this because most graduate students would not take this instructor's class so we had to rely on the notes and other information we collected during the year. When we saw the questions in our test package we knew our strategy had paid off for this professor. We were ready for this one. I wrote for four hours and it seemed that I had written over forty pages of information on this qual. This was the area that concerned me because of the many prima donnas teaching it. Also, the professor I challenged the summer before was going to correct the exams. Good thing the department was going through a little change so this professor's influence was diminishing. In the past he held the veto power over all doctoral students in this area. If he said yes you were anointed, but if he said no you were through. Apparently there were so many complaints about this professor that his prestige was diminishing and the procedures modified. He retired a year later, but should have retired many years earlier.

The next qual was in the area of Educational Sociology. I felt very comfortable in this area because I had done a lot of research for my Masters several years earlier. The exams were given to us and we began the writing session. I took a little over four hours on this one because a monitor came for our papers shortly after that time.

The last qual had to do with statistics. This was a difficult one for me but our research professor had prepared us for this. We took our calculators to the testing area (something that was prohibited before) and started the fourth and last qual. I was not too comfortable with this area (even though I got A's in the courses) but I wrote and used that calculator. I finished before the allotted time of four hours so I redid all my calculations and double-checked all my written information. I left before the end of the four hours but my friends stayed a long time after. It was almost two hours later that the top student in our class finished and arrived to have dinner with us. They all said that was the hardest test that they had ever taken, yet I felt that it was the easiest that I had. I thought for sure that I had blown that test because I was the first in our group to finish. A week went by when I received a letter from the Dean of the School of Education. I was so nervous I had my wife open and read the letter. It read that I had successfully passed all the quals and that I could proceed on to the dissertation stage. I actually was so full of emotion that I cried. At first it was hard to believe that I had passed all the examinations. Later I discovered that I was one of three out of ten who took the tests that passed all the examinations. I felt very good and I was certainly happy that I had studied so hard.

I was to find out the hard way how at the university level politics is very strong. I went to the Chairman of the Education Department for some guidance. Instead of insisting that he be my dissertation chairman, I allowed him to assign me to someone in the continuing education department. It seemed logical at the time, but that was a drastic error on my part. Several things were happening at the graduate school, and one was a move to get rid of this particular professor because he was just vegetating and non-productive. If I had known this, I would have really insisted on another chairman. Well, I met with him to discuss my first three chapters written early in October of 1973. I tried in vain to have meetings with him, but he was so evasive that I didn't meet with him until early January of 1974. I didn't have the good sense to check with the Dean of Education because I felt the chairman should be the one to show some leadership. I then took my three chapters to individuals on the committee. Another mistake. They tore it apart and referred me back to my chairman. After finally getting a meeting with my chairman and reviewing the proposal, we decided to take it to the full committee. The chairman assured me that he had the approval of the members of the committee so this would be a piece of cake. We finally got the

Julius C. Manrique, Ed.D.

group together on May 5th in the Dean of Graduate Studies office. The Dean asked the Chairman a few questions that he could not answer or defend. Then he proceeded to cut the proposal to shreds. By this time other members started to join in and I was completely lost. They rejected the proposal and the questionnaire which was the main part of the dissertation. I was emotionally distressed and I felt sick. All the work that had gone into this proposal went down the drain in a few minutes. There was no way I could salvage any part of this proposal. I went home and tried to pull myself together before telling my wife. I just cried because this was more than I could bear at the time. This seemed like the end of my educational career and such a waste all because of the politics at the graduate level. They fired the chairman of my committee and left me hanging. The day of infamy for me was at hand.

31. Moving Up?

In the spring of 1973 when the position at the junior college opened up, I witnessed politics at that level also. I applied for the position as an assistant dean of continuing education and the principal of the evening high school. This position had two employers, and it displayed some very fine cooperation between two districts. Sixty-five people applied for this job and the committee screened them down to five people who were interviewed. It was interesting that the composition of this committee was half from the college and the other from the city schools. They were deadlocked because the other individual, by the way, was a favorite of the superintendent and a member of the old boys network. Finally, a political ploy was concocted by the chairman of the committee. Since I was to be physically located at the college, it was decided that all the deans with whom I would work would make their recommendation to the president and the superintendent. Well, I didn't hear from the chair for several days and I thought that I was not selected.

One afternoon, my wife went to the elementary school to pick up our daughter, and the principal congratulated her about my new position. The other person who was a close friend of this principal had told him that he was not selected and that "Manrique" got the job. It is kind of funny very few people ever call me by my first name—always the last one! When I returned home from the university that evening my wife told me this, and again I began to wonder about personnel practices at both districts or why was it that I was always hired the hard way. I was beginning to feel that my race and nationality had a lot to do with it because I was a threat to the boys in the network. They wanted their kind and made it very difficult for anyone outside that little clique to get a chance at a higher paying and responsible position.

Apparently the college was to inform me, but they thought that the city schools were going to do it. Well, that evening I called the chair of the committee and told him what had happened. He immediately called the president of the college and shortly after he called me and apologized for the miscue. He was a very fine man and I enjoyed having him as my supervisor and president. After the first mix-up I received my first contract with the college and the city schools to work at this level. This would give me well-rounded professional experience and I would later work very hard for a very allusive position. The working conditions at the college level were ideal in the Fall of 1973. Things were falling into place after years of tears, toiling and frustrations. Little did I know at that time that politics again would affect my tenure and retirement at the college.

32. The Trip with Children

We purchased a new car in the Spring of 1974 and decided to take a four week vacation from all the turmoil and problems that we had during the last year (1973 – 1974). We just had to get away from Modesto and my job. During the month of July, we took a trip to Toronto and the lake where my wife's parents lived. Each year we would fly back for a few weeks, but this year we decided to drive and see the country. We headed north to Ashland, Oregon, to see some old friends of ours, then to Crater Lake, Yellowstone National Park, the Black Hills, Sioux City Falls, Lavonia, Michigan, Niagara Falls, and finally Toronto and Balsom Lake. We spent two good weeks relaxing at the lake, then we started back through Michigan, Ohio, Indiana, Kentucky, Tennessee, Arkansas, Texas, New Mexico, Arizona and back to Modesto. We covered about eight thousand miles on the road that summer. One thing we all learned was that we have a big country. There were some very beautiful spots in our country and every state has its beauty and fine points.

Our girls got the feel of the country, but I wondered how much they got out of the trip because they either slept or were very bored with the whole trip. At the beginning they seemed interested, but towards the end of the trip everything, including the Grand Canyon, was just OK. I have often wondered about the parents who go through these trips for their children? Who really benefits more? I sure hope the parents do because from what I can gather, some children sure don't. The trip went along well with the exception of the oil problem in the brand new Pontiac. For a new car it used too much oil. Later, it took much convincing off the dealer to fix the engine so it would not use that much oil. It was the last time I would buy a Pontiac or, for that matter, an America car.

33. The Doctorate

I returned to my position at the college in the Fall of 1974 ready and willing to work as hard as possible my first year at my new position at the Junior College. In the meantime, I called the Chairman of the School of Education at the University of the Pacific and made an appointment with him. We sat down, and I explained the situation and he told me my former chairman had been fired and he had returned to the East Coast. I got the feeling that they needed an excuse to fire him, and I was used as the catalyst to start the ball rolling, proving that he was incompetent. I was furious inside but I held my tongue and feelings because the chairman would be the only one I could rely on to complete my doctoral program. I sat calmly and we went over my proposal and the questionnaire that was dismantled early in May. We made a few technical changes here and there and he said," that should do it. Bring back five copies and then I'll share it with the other members of the committee." We reorganized a new committee in five minutes. We dropped three of the original ones and added three that he felt would be very helpful this time around. He would chair this proposal and he would keep the other members informed of the progress. I went home elated—what a difference the right person can make to one's future. I rewrote the first three chapters and the questionnaire exactly as he wanted it. I hand-carried them back to him within a month. He gave copies to the other members of the committee and got their approval for the questionnaire. I visited each member of the committee and asked if they were satisfied and that if the three chapters met their approval. They all said yes and signed off. We never met again until the final oral defense to be held on May 6, 1975. My chairman gave the go ahead with the questionnaire which was administered during the first two weeks of the Spring semester of 1975. The procedure was very smooth, and I thought that something might go wrong again, but, with the exception of a few lost questionnaires, they were all turned in on time. He assured me that he wanted me to complete the dissertation before May 6, 1975. It took me about three weeks to get all the questionnaires back from the staff. I had received permission from the president of the college to administer the questionnaire randomly to thirty-five instructors. They were very cooperative, and I thought I had something that would really help the college if they used the findings. Unfortunately, like most studies of this nature, it was completely ignored and it was never referred to during any administrative or staff meeting that I ever attended. I often wondered why but I never made any comments about it. I learned later that you have to give others in higher positions of authority recognition for your work in order to move up the educational ladder. Several individuals I was working for did not want me to move up the ladder. I was the first high-level Mexican-American administrator of the college.

I took the data to the chairman of the research department at the University of the Pacific. This was a real coincidence because my Mother's last name was the same as his. The chairman of the research department took my data cards which were ready for the computer and designed a program. This professor did extraordinary things for graduate students, and my respect really grew for him. He was similar to the previous chairman but in a quiet and less dramatic way. We finally got the program together after a few weeks, and then he ran the material. It seemed like months before the printouts were ready; however, they finally arrived on April 8th (my birthday). I took a week off from my job and worked with the research director to extrapolate the most cogent points from the mass of information that I had to work with. The study revealed many things about the college, but since the college was riding high with increased enrollment and everything at that point looked rosy, my study was not given any attention at all. This kind of bothered me, but I found out later that most dissertations are only important to those who write them because our educational system is proliferated with educational research. I spent hours and hours writing that fourth chapter which had to do with the statistical data necessary for the final chapter that presented the conclusions, findings and recommendations. My wife was a brilliant assistant during these crucial days. She did all the typing and editing for this piece of work. I look back and wondered if it would have been completed without her help. Well, we finally put the last two chapters together and gave the copies to my chairman. He studied them and made a few changes and then gave the approval to go ahead with the completion of the dissertation. He said "put it all together and have five copies ready for me on April 30, seven days before your oral defense." I had to develop an abstract so it could be announced to the entire university staff that I would be defending my dissertation on May 6th. Anyone could come and listen. Normally, many members of the various departments would come and ask questions on this subject, but I was one of the fortunate ones to have only my committee show up for this event. One of the original members of my committee could not be there, and for a long time I wondered why. The only reason I can deduce is that he could not face me after what he had done to me the year before. He did tell the chairman that if he approved the dissertation that he would sign it also.

So there I was at 2 p.m. on May 6, 1975, armed with information about my dissertation that I could defend for hours if I had to. I entered the room rather nervously remembering what had happened before, sat down, and introduced myself and the dissertation. I could hardly speak and my voice was cracking for about five minutes until I finally gained a little confidence, and I could see that this was a friendly group of men who wanted me to succeed. They didn't have any axes to grind with me or other members of the committee—not like before when they had it in for my previous chairman. It was rather easy from that point on to respond and present answers to all of their questions that were being asked. The time flew by, and then I was asked to leave the room while the four members made up their minds about my dissertation and defense. The ten-minute wait seemed like hours, but I was called in, and I was told all the members approved, and they would recommend to the School of Education to confer the doctorate. It was one of the happiest moments of my life. I drove home, and I couldn't wait to tell my wife and children.

The graduation ceremony was to take place on May 20th, just a few days away. Another surprise was that my wife's parents were coming out for a short visit, and they would be at the graduation ceremony. My office staff prepared a beautiful surprise party for me, and later the administrators had a campus affair honoring me for my accomplishments. The night of the graduation a few very close friends attended the ceremony. I took my relatives, my brother took my mother, Dr. and Mrs. Beamish, and Mr. and Mrs. Leon Lafaille went on their own. They all met at my home after the ceremony for a little champagne. These individuals were special people in my life.

First, my mother (and father) always wanted a Doctor in the family, and even though I had a doctorate in education, it was the closest I could come to being an M.D. She was seventy-five years old and didn't quite understand what this all meant, but she repeated over and over, Oh, how happy your dad would be if he were here! Yes, it was quite an accomplishment for one of her nine living sons who were born in dire poverty and destined to be a farm laborer to achieve the highest degree in education on a Ford Fellowship no less! You could see in her eyes and the way she embraced everyone that this too was one of her happiest moments. Little did we know that two years later she would have a stroke which would severely impair her dancing and arm movements, and the following winter she would leave us forever. But, at that moment she was her natural self: laughing, alert to questions, poking fun at a few people, moving around the room and just plain enjoying herself. I really think she had more happiness in her heart than the whole family put together. She would try to make me smile and would always encourage me to be happy, but for some reason or the other I was always a very serious individual and would reserve my happy moments for occasions like this one.

My brother Joe and his wife were there. I invited him because as we were growing up we always had some heated political discussions. He would always kid me that I was being taught by some professors at college that were Communist. This would really strike the wrong cord with me because some of the professors that I had were on the other end of the spectrum. He didn't graduate from high school, but he had a very good mind; always thinking and quite analytical. He wanted an education in the worst way but never put his best foot forward to work for it, but he was quite proud of what I had done. I mention him because as I was struggling through college my senior year I ran out of money and I couldn't find a job anywhere. I really didn't know where my next meal was coming from and it appeared that I would have to drop out another quarter. I remember going to the Student Services Office at the college to ask for a loan. I made an appointment to see the Dean and waited for hours before they called me in. It was my turn for a conference, but I couldn't ask anyone for a loan, and I left the building and went to my apartment. I really had no one to turn to, and I went home that weekend with a friend. Joe was there and he could tell I was deeply troubled. I told him I was broke, and he immediately gave me twenty dollars. This would last me a month and in the meantime I found a job to earn a little money so I could finish the semester. Please keep in mind I was living in an apartment where I paid $10.00 a month and I spent $5.00 a week on groceries. This seems incredible but it was the only way I could make it through school.

Mr. and Mrs. Leon Lafaille were there for two reasons. The first, he was my associate at work, but the real reason was that he was my health education instructor while I attended the first two years of college. He was one man who really impressed me as a sincere and hard-working college teacher. As was mentioned earlier in the book, his trust in me was displayed when my essay mysteriously disappeared from his office. I had two witnesses who saw me put it there, and it "walked off." My final grade depended upon it, and he believed me and gave me an "A" in the class. I never had forgotten that display of honesty and sincerity, and now I was working with him. It was a great feeling having him at my graduation ceremony because it proves that one never knows how much you can influence someone else just by being yourself.

The next couple was Dr. and Mrs. Jerome Beamish. They were two very close friends whom we met at a scouting dinner in Merced in the early 1960s. He was the director of guidance and professor at California State University, Stanislaus, and she was a budding artist in her own right. They were both from eastern Canada, so my wife had a lot in common with them. We became very close friends, and we would see each other frequently. Dr. Beamish was the individual who encouraged me to apply for the Ford Fellowship. He handed me the application one day in November of 1971, and I completed all the questions and returned it to New York. I did not hear from the Ford Foundation until the following March of 1972. My wife telephoned me at Tuolumne Elementary School where I was Principal that we had received a special delivery letter. She opened it, and it indicated that I had received a full fellowship and I could go to any university I wanted. I had to notify them immediately. I was just dumbfounded because I had never won a thing in my life. He was really responsible for me in returning to school that following year.

My wife's parents were proud that I had accomplished this tremendous education feat. They both knew the true value of an education and how important it was to be in the field. My father-in-law had an excellent mind and reminded me of my father. The major differences were that my father could not visualize his opportunities when they came and he could not save any of his earnings. I am sure with such a large family that was difficult, but if he had, our lives may have been different. So much depends on parents' attitude toward life in order to provide an example for their children. I found out that regardless of what I did, my two daughters would end up doing something different because our values and hardships really meant nothing to them. Well, my father-in-law and I hit it off very well and we had many enjoyable discussions together. My mother-in-law had graduated from high school and went to work immediately to support her parents. She was an intelligent woman and her mind was quick as a flash. She knew how to rear a family and save for a rainy day with the income that the both of them had. Both of these people had many hard and difficult times during their marriage, but they held together and had many wonderful retirement years together. I wanted to emulate some of their ideas about life, and I was very happy they were here at my graduation ceremony.

My wife had prepared a few items to eat and we enjoyed some champagne toasts. She was extremely proud, and I said to myself many times later—how could I ever repay her for all of her help and sacrifice? Here was a brilliant woman who gave up almost everything and almost all of her friends to help her husband? How many men ever take the time to realize the sacrifice many women make for their husbands. I realized this and tried to encourage her to go back to school to receive her Masters and Doctorate. She could do it easily only if she were not so obligated and dedicated to help give our daughters and family the best possible living environment we could possibly have. She was a voracious reader and had a quick mind like her mother. It appeared that she would always be at my side through thick and thin. Our two daughters were there but could not really fathom how important this occasion was to me or the family. They were two bright and fine looking girls, and they went everywhere we went.

The evening ended and our guests left. I received many cards of congratulations from many of my acquaintances and former students when my name was published in various newspapers. I had reached the apex of my educational career by receiving the doctorate degree. I was so proud that when people called me Dr. Manrique, I would blush a little. It had a different ring to it, but I enjoyed it. The glow would wear off very soon because many of my professional peers would never call me by my title and they would even slight me now and then. There were only four earned doctorates on the administrative staff at the time but some administrators never referred to me by my title, but the other three were always called by their title because of their positions. This bothered me a little, but I soon realized that wherever you went there would always be petty jealousy. Many would tell me, "Oh, I could have gotten my doctorate, but I didn't want to put my family through that sacrifice," or "I could have gotten my doctorate, but it doesn't mean that much to me or that I am an A.B.D" (All But Dissertation), and "just never found the time to complete the program" or "What good is an Ed.D. at this level? It's not going to do you any good," and many more excuses, and complaints. These same people never did concede that it took a tremendous amount of perseverance, initiative, intelligence, and sacrifice to complete the program in three years. This gave more credence to an idea I had about the attitude of education and our peers. This started a series of events that almost made me leave the education profession. The higher one goes into the educational field, the harder one finds it is to tolerate some of the biases and prejudices that are very prevalent. I influenced many people to try for their doctorates, directly and indirectly, but many would never give me credit for that. A few unethical educators made the comment that "if Manrique can get a doctorate, anyone can." One could feel the bias and underlying feeling with a statement like that. I was always quite polite and unresponsive to comments like that.

34. Climbing the Educational Ladder

I have always been a hard worker and I have always respected my professional peers, but as the school years moved on I began to change my attitude a little. My teaching career started at the eighth grade level in Oakdale, California. I had never really suffered directly from bias or prejudice because of my Mexican-American background. In all my years in this profession I never once used my nationality in order to obtain a higher position. Affirmative action would never have been enacted if those in the hiring positions were sincere, fair, and honest in their hiring practices. When I started looking for a teaching position in Stanislaus County in 1955 some people thought I was crazy because there were no native Mexican-American teachers in the county. I immediately found out how prejudiced administrators were. I remember going to the one of the administrative offices looking for a position and met the assistant superintendent. He told me of a position that was open at a Junior High and asked me to go and see the principal. I took him seriously and made an appointment to see the principal. This was my first attempt at seeking a job one of many to follow before I arrived at a satisfying position. I saw the principal (an Anglo), and we sat down and the usual questions followed. He didn't seem too interested in me and asked me who was the president of the Yosemite Area Council in 1948. I had no idea who he was talking about, but later I realized how important the answer to that question was. You see, in those days community service was almost required of each teacher, and if you were connected with the scouting movement you were destined to stardom and a higher position in the district because the top administrators in the district were pro-scouting. I heard later that the position I interviewed for was filled and that the principal wouldn't have hired a "Mexican" unless they forced him.

Little did I know then that, ten years later, I was hired as vice principal of that same school, and that I forced the resignation of that principal because he didn't want to work with a Mexican. I later went to the Stanislaus County Superintendent of Schools office to find out if there were any openings in the county schools. He said there was an opening in Turlock and one in the Sylvan School district. I did not go to Turlock because that city was lily-white in the first place, and there wasn't a chance in hell for anyone other that a white person getting a job in that school district. I made an appointment with the superintendent of the Sylvan school district, and we sat down to talk. We went through the same ritual as with the other officials. The conference lasted about fifteen minutes, and he said there was no position available at that time and that he would call me if something comes up. Was he telling truth? Until this day twenty-odd years later, I have never heard from that superintendent. My brother had children going to school in that district and he told me that they did hire a social studies teacher for their oldest son's class. I was beginning to see how the system worked—you had to know the "right people" before you could get a job in this county or maybe anywhere? I met that superintendent again when I ran for the Stanislaus County Superintendent position because he strongly supported my opponent. I really heard from him and how he felt about me and my nationality. Have you ever heard people say, "Hey, I'm not prejudice, some of my best friends are Mexicans." Just ask them how many times they have asked these "friends" over for dinner and that ends the conversation regarding "Mexican friends." So many so-called leaders of the community are very superficial or political and make these comments when seeking votes, but in the back rooms they sing a different tune (recall the Texaco CEOs). Many racial slurs are made behind closed doors when the boys are playing their monthly game of cards—they let it all hang out (some record it). Many of the so-called friends of the minorities are not really helpful to their causes even though they walk in some of their marches. I guess the lower middle and middle class are the ones who are quite open about their prejudices; but the upper class, the ones in power, have a little different and subtle way of showing their biases.

That year I decided to finish my education and get my credential and be fully qualified for any job available. I thought I would try to seek a position in my hometown. I happened to know this superintendent and went to see him at his home during Christmas vacation. When I rang the doorbell he came to the door and looked at me with quite a puzzled look. He didn't recognize me. I introduced myself; then he remembered. I didn't have a tie on nor was I dressed formally which may have made a difference. I asked him about the job opening and he said, "Julius, we don't have any janitor jobs available, and it may be some time before we have one." I kind of choked a little and said I was a credentialed teacher, and I was looking for a teaching position. He immediately said that all the position had been filled. This conversation took place outside in the cold and he never once invited me in to his home. With his face quite red, I excused myself, and I never ever went back to his home even though I worked later for the district more that eight years.

Why did I want a job in my home county or city so badly? Why? Why? Only a poor minority would have the answer to that—to prove the power structure wrong about minorities. We are not inferior and predestined to menial tasks if we are given the opportunity to succeed at different jobs. I didn't have the answer to that question when I started my career, but that idea got stronger and stronger all throughout my career.

Well, with those early experiences in looking for a job, I stopped and decided to wait until the spring before I would try again. My neighbor was a teacher and told me they needed substitutes at the local high school, and he encouraged me to sign up for a job. Well, I had nothing to lose, so I did. It just so happened that the Asian flu was running rampant that year and I was fortunate to be hired as a full-time substitute at the local high school. I actually got paid for doing something I liked. I taught almost every subject and I really hit it off well with the students. I was just a few years older than most seniors—twenty-three years old. I worked over a month at this school and then I was asked to teach a seventh grade mathematics class at the elementary school. This was beautiful and I filled in for a teacher the rest of the school year. My classroom management and discipline were my strong suits along with my desire to teach the students something.

The superintendent (the one that told me that he had no janitorial jobs available) came by my class one afternoon and asked if I would be interested in teaching a social studies class at the eighth grade level (the same class that I was taught social studies as a student there). I didn't think it over too long because jobs were not available at this time, and the luck that I had I better take this one. I know I was the first and only native Mexican-American teacher hired at the all white school staff, and I was the only native born Mexican-American hired in the whole county at that time. This was a first, and years later under "affirmative action" school districts were forced to reluctantly hire, not only Mexican-Americans, but also blacks and other minorities. It took me a little time to realize that I would be making $4,000.00 a year and working in a nice, clean, warm and respected position. What honor this would bring to my family! Some members of the white establishment couldn't believe that it was possible that the Mexican from the East Side of the tracks could teach their children social studies. I was watched with a "jaundiced eye," and I am sure I was monitored very closely by the board and the principal without me knowing it.

The best public relations teachers could have are their students. You send them home happy and with zeal to learn, your battle with the parents will be nil. I drew on many of my sad experiences as a student to make my classroom the happiest, cleanest, nicest, most serious, and most productive in the whole school. Even though there was chaos down the hall or next door, my classroom was to be the one that students wanted to come to and learn. The superintendent said of me later, Julius' classes were desired by all students, and even those in the lower grades were just eager to enter his room, and they were reluctant to leave —"it was quite a learning environment." After all those years, I later wondered why I remained eight years at my first assignment when I had opportunity at different levels and other school districts. I remained because I had to prove to the community and the power structure and to myself that I could be an outstanding teacher and person. I guess this matters when you are struggling and trying to find your place in the world, but sometimes as in my father's case opportunities slip by you and never come again. I found this out later in life.

After eight years in Oakdale and without any mentors, encouragements or future in that district, I moved to Modesto. I got a job at one of the roughest junior high schools in the district at that time—Mark Twain. I had very few problems with the students there and it was the first time I had taught in a racially mixed school, other than my student teaching at San Jose. The principal noticed and evaluated me periodically and then encouraged me to get an administrative credential because he saw in me the potential of a good administrator. This was the first time any person took me aside and gave me some good advice. I didn't realize why he did this until much later. We had a similar godfather in the district, and apparently he told my principal to encourage me to go on because a principalship would be opening up in the near future. I did go back to school to pick up my administrative credential, but then the following year I received an appointment at Grace Davis High School. This would give me the secondary experience that I needed for future interviews. My godfather was looking after me. After a year at the high school, I received my vice-principalship at Roosevelt Junior High (the same place where the principal refused me several years earlier and resigned because he did not want to work with a Mexican). I worked at that position for three years and then received an elementary principalship with additional experiences to broaden my educational background. Now I had elementary, junior high, high school, and junior college experiences to help me with future positions in the district, but a tragedy occurred. My godfather was in a serious accident on the way home from a board meeting and was put out of action for some time. When he recovered, he was not able to resume his full-time work. In the meantime, the superintendent retired and the board selected someone other than my godfather. He was crushed and retired, and that ended my climb up the ladder with this district. The new superintendent had a completely different philosophy than many of us subordinates, and we didn't hit it off too well. He was tough minded and liked controversy. That is how he started and that is how his career ended! Finally, it got so bad the district had to buy off his contract. My career ended with the city schools also when I became full-time employee at the Junior College.

35. Hard Bumps

If my educational godfather had become superintendent my whole educational career may have been different. Before I obtained any higher positions I would have many very sad and unethical experiences in education. I applied for the Dean of Boys position at one of the high schools, but I was never interviewed. My principal shared with me a conversation that he had with the newly appointed superintendent—he asked, "Is Julius ready?" My principal answered, "yes." I didn't get the job. I applied for a junior high principalship and no interviews were held and another vice principal got the nod. I went to the superintendent and asked why I was passed over—he said," I have to take a chance with somebody different." I waited two years before I applied for another 7-8 principalship. The interview went smoothly, and I thought I had it made. As a matter of fact, several people called me and congratulated me before the announcement was made. Apparently my name went to the board but one board member said, "Is that the best we can do?" More names were selected, and a K-6 Principal who was a fishing buddy of the assistant superintendent was selected. He lasted at that position three years, and the school was literally in chaos. He was sent back to the elementary level. This again told me that if you knew the "right people" you could get ahead even though you don't have the experience or educational skills.

One more try—when Beyer High School opened up they needed a vice principal. This was a classic example of the bias that I had seen in this district and probably occurs in others. I was given an interview the evening shortly after me and my wife had returned from a vacation in Hawaii. It was a rushed affair because they wanted to make the announcement the next day. The interview was really a farce. The principal of the school whom I thought was sincere and honest and a friend, was someone I helped run a junior high school for two years. Until that time, he had no administrative experience, but the curriculum director for the district and he collaborated on many district projects. This appointment as principal was his plum because he knew the right people. I received a letter from him the next day (apparently the letter was already in the mail the evening of the interview) saying "because of philosophical differences regarding educational matters, you were not chosen for this position." I could not believe this was happening to me. I had all the credentials, experiences, abilities, high ethical standards, ideas, and interest to help students in the community. What was wrong? Two things—my godfather was no longer influential and I was the only native Mexican-American administrator in the school district and the county. I never made noises about this, but I really should have. I also should have left the county, but my home was here. Later in my career, I was told by another prominent superintendent that "people vote with their feet." I got the message that my future was not here with this district. I took a leave of absence at the first opportunity because I was locked in, and I could not move vertically or horizontally with my educational career.

36. More Obstacles

Well, my experiences at the junior college were not that dramatic but there were some similarities and much more subtle. I thought that the politics of education would be different at this level, but I was wrong. I was hired as a part-time English As a Second Language instructor in 1961. This was a beautiful situation, and I taught twice a week for seventeen weeks, each semester, during the evening. I made four dollars an hour, and I was teaching in the evening. I would save this money and travel during the summer so I could grow professionally. I always encouraged my peers and my staff to travel and gain extra experiences which helped make their classes more interesting. I had a tremendous amount of zeal, interest, and desire to make the teaching profession a respected one, but as I moved along through life, this attitude and feeling diminished quite a bit. The main reason why I started to teach adults was because of an incident that happened to me while taking an adult class. I sat in this evening class three hours a night once a week, and I just wasn't getting a thing out of the instructor. He was a sad example of a college teacher, and I said to myself, "If that guy can teach here, anybody can." I dropped the class and went over to the Dean of Continuing Education and explained why I dropped. I left my name and credentials and said to him, "Anytime you need a good teacher for a difficult course, let me know." Little did I know that the following Spring semester I would receive a call from him asking me to teach and expand the English As A Second Language class. The program was just starting to expand so I was called in to develop the more advance course with another instructor. This was a class that gave the students the opportunity to learn how to speak English. This was a thrill for me to see the enthusiasm and desire of the adults to learn English. My classes had a little United Nations complexion throughout the year. I was deeply impressed with the caliber of the students and their attendance. Five years just zoomed by, and I thought it was time for a change. I then began teaching a conversational Spanish class. This was my minor in college, and I was putting my knowledge to work. This was a wonderful feeling to converse in my parent's language. My classes were always huge to start, but the attendance dropped off midway through the semester. The reason was simply that the students had to discipline themselves to learn a language and study, but many of them just couldn't. It was a little different situation with the English As A Second Language classes—those student remained in the class until the very end. I had a little different clientele in the Spanish classes, but I still enjoyed it. Five years rolled by, and I became quite busy with my principalship and various community activities, so I decided to step down to let a younger person take over. I told the dean that if he needed someone in administration someday to keep me in mind—he did.

Several years later, I was hired by the college as an Assistant Dean of Continuing Education/ Evening High school principal. My professional growth as an Assistant Dean of Continuing Education was quite a struggle because I attempted to enter a field where no black or Mexican-American was ever hired at this institution. My first attempt at this position was in 1967. There was no such thing as "affirmative action" for me, and all that was available was the old-fashioned system of being appointed by the right people. I did have a close friend in the system, but he was not at the district level. He was a third line manager, and he was a close friend whom I had known for many years. Little did I know he was pulling for me, but he was over-ruled many times because of the faculty leadership on the various committees and other deans who had much more influence than he. The first attempt for a junior college interview stands out in my mind very vividly. The interview was held in the South Hall in a dingy room with three people including my friend. The other two individuals asked some irrelevant questions, and the conference lasted about fifteen to twenty minutes. I knew I didn't have a chance when I left. One member of the committee was one that I had gone to school with, and I knew personally he did not like Mexicans. The other was the Dean of Instruction who was a Mormon—need I say more. I was told by my friend that I should socially cultivate these college people more and maybe even play golf with a few of them so they could get to know me better. Those were key words to me—

socialize, butter up, wine and dine, do anything to get your name in front of the "right people." I said to myself right then and there that I would never share my time or liquor for that purpose. Maybe that's why it took me so long to arrive at the various positions in life. My second attempt was in 1969. I had just been appointed principal of an elementary school, and an administrative position opened up at the college. The person that left was just interested in a temporary position at the college and left for a position in Hawaii. I talked to my close friend and the president of the college this time to let them know I was interested. However, our family had planned a railroad and automobile trip through Canada, so I left phone numbers of every place I was to be while we traveled across the country. I never heard a word from the screening committee which was headed by the Dean of Students. But I did hear from him indirectly that if I were really interested I wouldn't have gone on my trip.

I was shopping downtown one day after returning from our trip and ran into the president of the college. He asked where I was and he said, "We tried to get hold of you but couldn't." I told him that I had left the numbers where I could be reached with the dean's secretary. They interviewed one person and hired him. The college was to have several problems with him later, and the faculty would be upset because of his inability to function at this level. I was caught in a crossfire, so to speak, because my godfather at the city schools level wouldn't release me to go to the junior college and the Dean of Students wouldn't pull for me to come to the junior college, so they selected someone else. This was explained to me much later, and I wondered many times what the real reason was for not being hired at the college at that time. During my second year as principal of an elementary school, I was visited by the principal of the evening high school. He was told by my friend at the college to deliver the announcement of an opening at the college. His comment to me when he gave it to me was "if Mr. Jones (fictitious name) applies for the job you won't have a chance—it has already been decided that he will get the job." This really bothered me —why should I apply? Well, I did, and he was correct. I don't remember a thing about that interview, but I did remember Mr. Jones coming out of the door when I was coming into the building. When the committee started to ask me questions, I could feel that they were not even listening to my answers. The meeting lasted about forty-five minutes, and the chairman escorted me out of the room. Several days later, I received a form letter saying I was not chosen, and Mr. Jones was selected. I could see why he was chosen over me. He taught at the college for more than 20 years; he was the department chairman; and he was one of the most popular instructors on the campus. There were no ill feelings on my part when this person got the job because he was the best man for it. The appointment of the other two was a different story, and this really cemented my impression about biased leadership and the personnel practices at this level.

My next try at this level was in the Spring of 1973 when the Principal of the Evening High School and the Assistant Dean of Continuing Education retired (a combination position shared by the city schools and the junior college). Each district shared part of the salary but the position was housed at the Junior College. It was as unique position which was a leftover from the old adult school and governing board. The city schools wanted only the high school diploma program, and the junior college took the adult portion that included all the non-credit courses in the adult area. I can't remember how I found out about the opening because I was on leave of absence, working on my Doctorate at the University of the Pacific at the time. I applied along with sixty-five others, and I was one of six to have the opportunity for an interview. I felt my chances were very slim, but I went through the motions once again. The composition of the committee was very interesting. There were four members representing the city schools and four members representing the junior college, plus the chairman. I was out of touch with almost everyone that year because of my studies, but several friends (really acquaintances) called me and told me who had applied from the district. When I found out, my feeling for the interview was sustained. I had to really sway the junior college representatives because the city schools representatives were definitely favoring a former junior high school principal who had been a favorite of the assistant superintendent and the superintendent. His major problem was his age—he was about to retire in a few years. I was called in for the interview and immediately I could tell by the line of questions that the city schools' representatives were trying very hard to find some weaknesses in my qualifications. For instance, the assistant superintendent asked me about my qualifications to counsel adults. I realized I didn't have a Pupil Personnel Credential, but I had a general administrative credential which supersedes the former. I also mentioned that I had counseled adults while teaching them for the past ten years in the evening program. I mentioned how I could or would counsel them and how I helped in the community. He did finally ask me if I had a Pupil Personnel Credential, and I answered no. Each time the questions from the city schools representatives were used to find a weakness in my qualifications. The members from the college elicited answers which proved my competency and knowledge about the junior college system. I thought they were fair, but the others were certainly not. The interview lasted more that an hour, and I was exhausted when it was over. I felt the committee would not choose me. A week went by, and I received a call from the committee chairman. The committee was deadlocked (4-4) with the chairman favoring me, but he wanted the top two to have another interview with the deans, assistant deans, President of the College, etc. with whom they would be working at the college. The other person was the former junior high principal and a very close friend of the assistant superintendent. I felt my chances were a little better with all the junior college administrators, including the president, on the final reviewing committee. I was introduced to them by the chairman, and for an hour I answered questions. As I was about to leave, a member of the committee asked me if I ever got mad at staff members. I hesitated because it was a leading question and one that I could explain either way I answered it. I said yes, and off I went giving reasons why. After I left the meeting, I told myself I really blew that one by answering that last question. I didn't hear from the committee for several weeks, but my wife was visiting a school where our daughters attended, and the principal of off-handedly said, "Congratulations for Julius are due, aren't they?" My wife looked stunned and said, "What do you mean?" He said, "You haven't heard? Mr. White (fictitious name) didn't get the job and they chose Julius over him." My wife told him we hadn't heard yet, and thanked him. Later I called the chairman and he apologized for the President because a letter was supposed to have been sent a week ago confirming that I was selected for the position. I felt happy yet sad because I had to go through every hurdle possible. Was it the color of my skin, qualifications, personality, social status, politics or my inability to cultivate the "right people" that prevented me from advancing up the educational ladder?

37. Hard Work Doesn't Do It

This made me work harder and made me more determined than ever to obtain that doctorate, California Community College Chief Administrative and Student Workers Personnel Credentials. I didn't want to be under-qualified for any position that I would attempt in the future. I found out the hard way that you need to have contacts (network, today) and friends pulling for you all the way before you could make it to the top and you mustn't make anyone angry because they may be on that committee interviewing you next time. My friend at the junior college fell in disfavor (just as my godfather at the city schools did), and he had lost his influence which in turn did not help me. I didn't read the political winds quickly enough, and my chances for further opportunity at this college were becoming very slim. Several very cruel and unethical events happened to me which convinced me about the politics of higher education. I was called into the President's office and told I was going to be appointed assistant dean of instruction and I would come aboard full time. We were to meet with the superintendents of both school districts to make this announcement. The dean of instruction was so happy, she called me late one Friday night and wanted to celebrate with a bottle of champagne. She needed help in the worst way because she had so many people reporting to her and she was new at the job. Her position was never advertised nor were there any interviews held for that position—she was a woman and a good person, so the superintendent didn't object, but the leadership of the faculty did. The board approved her with no problem, and they even praised the decision—first woman to ever have that position. What happened to "affirmative action" and all the interviews that some people have to go though? This happens often in education—everyone in the system knows who has the job before the board or the public. For instance, many school district personnel officers will say they are scouring the nation for a replacement and announce that 50, 100 or 200 applications have been received for one job and how difficult it was to select five or six for interviews. All this charade goes on when the interviewing committee knows who will be selected or whom the board wants as their appointee. Some would say "that is politics" and others would say "that smells of old cronies" —but that is the way it is!

The following Friday the president and the superintendent had a meeting with the city schools superintendent. This had been arranged for months, and out of the blue the president called me to tell me that because of financial problems with both districts he would not ask that I be appointed as assistant dean of instruction as he had told me several weeks before. I was to go with him and the superintendent and discuss with the city schools superintendent that they could not bring me aboard full time just yet and that they wanted to leave things as they were for the moment. I sat there in this office with men who were making double my salary, and they could not afford to bring on board another half-time person costing the districts very little out of a budget of twenty million or more dollars (at that time). I couldn't believe what was happening to me. Where were the feelings of these individuals? Were they really trying to crush me? What did I do to be treated in this manner? What about their personnel practices? Did these practices favor only the white or the most vocal black or Chicano? I never did find out exactly what the problem was to not give me the opportunity to go up the ladder, but I did find out later that these two superintendents had very big egos, wanted no competition, and once you crossed them, no matter how small, they never forgot. This was payback time for something I said or did—but for the love of me I could not remember.

I left the office, and the three men talked on as if nothing had happened. I knew then I had to leave the city, county, and the state, so I started to seek job openings from all over. I applied for positions for which I really wasn't qualified or that I knew I wouldn't even get a chance to be interviewed. This was done strictly out of frustration. I was wild with anger that something was wrong, but no one had the professional courtesy to tell me. All my credentials and letters of recommendation were in order but not even a nibble or a chance to prove myself.

A year passed, and finally the Dean of Students decided to go back to full-time counseling. I had the qualification plus an earned doctorate, so I applied. The personnel office wrote the job description for an individual who had been a counselor (this was common practice in some districts) and had a pupil personnel credential. Well, I had been a counselor at the junior high level, and I had the Student Workers Credential which made me qualified. Several people applied, and I was selected for an interview. I was the last because I had taken a vacation in Oregon, and I just returned. I worked like hell that summer as Summer School Director and I had to take a few days off. That summer I had three days of vacation and the evening I got back they wanted to interview me (similar to the vice principal position the day I returned from Hawaii). I felt something smelly already, but what the hell, I was ready to go through this farce. I could sense something was wrong the minute I walked into the conference room. The Chairman who was a former speech teacher was so nervous he could hardly talk or even look at me. He muttered a few words and then asked me to introduce myself. This was ridiculous because everyone in that room knew my life history. There was one man in the room who was about to retire called the "gray fox." He got his position only because he knew the "right people" not because of his intelligence or ability. He didn't have a formal degree, no Masters, but he made it to the top, because when the junior colleges split with the high schools, he got in on the ground floor. I knew he was against me because his golfing buddy had applied also. He had made a statement to me that I have never forgotten. "I've worked many nights to get where I am, and I'll see to it that others will do the same." He was a little jealous of my doctorate and of me for applying for this position when I had been with the district only a few years. He was going to make sure that I toiled very hard before moving up the ladder. The other administrator was the finest person I had ever met at this college as a student and as employee. However, he played golf with the silver fox and the other, so they pretty well knew whom they were going to select. There was a secretary on the committee that asked the most asinine question that I still remember—"What do you see as the worst problem in the world?" How relevant was this question for the job that I was applying for? I should have challenged this interview in court because they didn't follow any "affirmative action guidelines." The reading skills department was represented by a woman who wanted to protect that area, and her questions had to do with student skills for the college level. Her background had been purely elementary school, but somehow she was a good reading teacher at the college level. The last member of the committee was a young man who represented the counseling department. He was a mixed up man already having married, divorced, remarried one of his students, and acted much like a pseudo-psychologist. His questions to me were—"What counseling books have you read recently?" I had just finished my dissertation and finished reading hundreds of books on student personnel so I rattled off a dozen or so. I was never impressed with the counseling services at any level, but at this level it was something else. A few made it very bad for the majority because they worked the least amount of time, and they were constantly complaining about the working conditions.

The interview lasted about forty-five minutes, and then I left feeling sick. That was the second biggest farce that I had ever experienced. There were no questions regarding the job, and I immediately wrote down the questions that they had asked. Not one pertains to the job description—should I contest it? I thought about it and decided not to—what is the use? I saw my personal friend in the office the next day and asked him how I did? He said, great! I asked if I were number one? He hesitated and said, "We're sending the names to the President alphabetically." He was a quick thinker, but I couldn't believe what I had heard. My name began with an M and the other person's name began with an L; therefore, I didn't get the job. He later came by my office and tried to console me but the damage had been done. The following Tuesday the President at 8 a.m. called me in to give the bad news. I entered his office and with his back to me said, "Manrique I am recommending Mr. Long (fictitious name) for the position, and I will announce it to the faculty at today's meeting." What kind of man was this to give with one hand and then take with the other? I was deeply hurt, and I had a hard time recovering from that blow. I acted a little differently for several days and weeks afterwards because I was angry at the system and the process. Working hard really doesn't matter, it is knowing "the right people" and being at the right place at the right time. This was to happen again, but that time I was too close to retirement "to vote with my feet" as the superintendent had told me several years earlier.

I threw myself into project after project and worked and worked to try to forget this sordid affair. I knew I had to leave somehow, so again I started to apply for various positions. This time with a little more care and skill. I was invited for an interview over along the coast. It was a beautiful school and had a decent interview. I wrote the President after and told him so. It was for the dean of instruction position which was the next logical step for me. I was not selected, but I was sent a nice "Dear John" letter. I had another interview for the vice president position in charge of instruction at a junior college in the foothills. It seemed like a good situation and a fair interview. As I was waiting for the interview, the retiring vice president came by the room and handed me a dittoed list of questions on it. He couldn't resist saying, "By the way, you were not on the first ten names to be interviewed —we had to dig further to get you." I knew what that meant—another farce. And then he left with a big smile on his face. I didn't let that bother me and plunged right into the questions. It was a large committee of ten and fairly well balanced, but the department chairman was well in command. Many of their questions had to deal with governance of the college. I was satisfied with the interview, but in the back of my mind, I knew I wouldn't be selected. I guess all my experiences up to this time gave me a clear indication of my chances with different committees. I thought I handled all the questions well, and the committee seemed to be listening to what I had to say. Well, I received a very nice "Dear John" letter telling me who got the position and why the committee selected him. That was probably the best "Dear John" letter I have ever received from anyone. I appreciated their comments and felt that the school had a little class and a fine personnel officer. After all these interviews, I felt I was locked into a very difficult situation. I couldn't move up in the ranks at either the junior college or administration at the K-12 area because I didn't have any direct administrative experiences. One had to attend conferences and make close contacts at different level and in different cities. I was beginning to learn that you cannot succeed in life without the help of someone else. With all the education, experience and community involvement that I had, I felt very much at a loss and very disappointed.

38. The Race and Consequences

Well, one last hope arrived, I thought! The Stanislaus County Superintendent (at that time) was in deep political trouble because of his handling of the Master plan for the handicapped students. It was mentioned constantly in the local newspapers. A few close friends of mine urged me to throw my hat into the ring, but I hesitated for many reasons. One is my ethnic background. Would the citizens of this racially biased county elect a Mexican-American to be their county superintendent? I knew a lot of people and many knew me—could it be possible? When a group of board members, and administrators met, in a so called "open meeting" to decide to select one of their own to run against the incumbent early in the Fall of 1977, I decided to challenge that "old boy network." I announced my candidacy, and it made the headlines. The first thing the local paper mentioned was that my father was a native of Mexico which clearly set the tone of other articles to follow regarding my background. No one else decided to announce until the following January, February, and March when there were nine candidates in the race. They all felt qualified for this position and threw their hats into the ring. In my honest opinion, there were only three qualified candidates, but the political race was on. My committee organized very well and financial contributions started to roll in. I felt very good about the prospect of being elected in the primary. Our group got the most signatures for the "in lieu of filing fee" petition—more than thirty-two hundred signatures. This large number defrayed most of the cost of the filing fee. The next big hurdle was the appointive versus the elective procedure for this office. Our committee worked hard for the elective procedure, because we knew that I would never be appointed by the ad hoc committee that would do the selecting. We opposed the editors of the local paper with a two hundred-word letter to the editor indicating the reasons for the elective process. This would be fatal for me because when it was time for an endorsement, the local paper endorsed someone else. The one presented by the appointive group was filled with grammatical errors and they had many very weak statements. It appeared on the elective ballot which proved to be another error for the elective office. They forgot to place a legal notice in the newspaper alerting the public that items could be placed in opposition the appointive view needed. Our committee was trying to be fair to the public and wanted the opportunity to respond. The local paper had already taken a stand in favor of the appointive process and the rationale was very weak. My name was tossed around as a "trouble maker" because I brought out some legal requirements that were not being met. Finally, the editorial board of the local paper gave our committee the opportunity to write up an article in favor of the elective position. They waited until the last minute to do so, and we spent many hours drawing up a draft. At 11 p.m., just twelve hours before the deadline, we turned in our response. It was a beautiful document which made the pro-appointive position look quite weak. We felt that this helped the overwhelming 3-1 voting in favor of the elective process, but it did not endear us to the editorial staff as we found out later. They would be the difference during the primary. The campaign was a rather mild one with most candidates showing respect for each other during the numerous open forums. These forums were never very well attended and then usually by special interest groups. I had quite a broad cross section of support with some of the most influential people in the community supporting me to the common worker in various walks of life. My contributions came in nicely, but some people really disappointed me. Some of my "friends" never got behind me to really make my campaign take off. We had a beautiful letter-writing campaign which consisted of many people who knew me personally and knew of all the things that I had done for the community. I got help from many parts of the county, and I felt very good about the progress until I saw how much money was being spent by a certain candidate. The candidates were an interesting group of people with very big egos.

I announced first in October of 1977 which gave many people the chance to determine if they were going to run against me. Many people felt I had a good chance, and others said my ethnic background would hurt. I had to find out if my belief in the American system of fair play was real or not. I wanted to see if a good, well-qualified, industrious, honest and ethical person could be elected to this position regardless of his ethnicity. It was never once mentioned by any candidate in the open, but members of my committee sure told me about the rumors that were being spread by some of the candidates. I don't think it was the final contributing factor why I didn't win, but it was one that turned the voters very easily in the county which had some subtle and sometimes open racial undertones. There were no top Mexican-American officials or school administrators in the county, and I wanted to be the first. The next person who announced his candidacy was an elementary school principal who had been in the city for about ten years. He lived in my general area and was responsible for taking many of my votes. He and another candidate just pounded the pavements in my hometown of Oakdale, my base of support, and took away the many votes I needed to win. He was an extrovert and had a very big ego. The next person who entered the contest was an employee of the county schools and the campaign was a disaster for him. The next person was an administrative assistant for the largest school district in the county. He was an unknown but by the end of the campaign he pulled out an upset over everyone. He outspent everyone and proved that if you spend enough money you can buy an election. His campaign had to be the most political because he lined up supporters from city hall and the power structure. There were many reasons why they supported him, and they were reluctant to give me any help. The next person was an elementary superintendent who knew the political ropes because he had been the chairman of the County Republican Party. He was a man in his early fifties and he had lived in the county some twenty-one years. He was very active in service and social clubs which really made the difference during the primary. The next two candidates announced their candidacy one day, and they found out they had no support so dropped out immediately. The last candidate to announce was an elderly superintendent who had the backing from supporters of a large church group. He also had no business being in this race, in my opinion. The last candidate was an assistant superintendent from a small school district on the west side of the county. He, of all the individuals, was the poorest and least prepared for the race. It was kind of like who was on first, no, he is on second, or third situations with so many candidates running. But I got the feeling, and it proved correct, that each of these individuals pulled voters from the base that I had cultivated.

We had an excellent committee on paper, but as in many situations the work fell upon me, my chairman and my wonderful wife. She kept the committee steady and ready for the problems that arose. The campaign went along with some minor problems, and things looked very favorable for me. I received many very favorable articles in the "letters to the editor" part of the local paper. These were not solicited, and I was sure that many more were sent but the local paper would not print them because they wanted to be fair to the other candidates. During the last two weeks of the campaign, only two letters favoring me were printed compared to fifteen letters favoring one of the favorites. Only after a series of questions by my committee to the editors did they finally publish a few more of mine. We knew there were many more that never even got noticed and probably found their way to the trash can. This election developed some very strong biased positions especially since Proposition 13 was also on the ballot. It was poor timing for me because it brought out all the malcontents and those that would never have voted in the first place. Our committee knew this would hurt me because of my non-Anglo-Saxon name. One learns so much from campaigning for a political office. You develop some strong allegiances and you find out who is your true friend even in your own family. My educational godfather was another reason why I lost this election. Remember how I described him helping me along through the educational ladder, well this all came to an abrupt halt a week before the election. He came out in favor of my opponent with a long, favorable letter to the editor.

There were two major reasons why he supported the other candidate. One was that I differed several times with what was happening in the scouting movement, and our philosophies clashed. Young bucks who wish to get ahead in any organization must never butt heads with the seniors who pack a lot of power and friends in the group. You are signing your own death warrant when you do that, and I did not realize that until it was too late. All I wanted to do is change some of the past practices that had gone on for years. I later remembered what this same person did to another aspirant of the Presidency of the Yosemite Council when his name came up for that position. This same individual black-balled him just by saying to the nominating committee, "I think he tips his elbow too much." That did it and that very nice individual never became anybody in the Yosemite Council.

The other one was more damaging. He was elected city councilman, and this changed his personality. He had retired from education and thought he could use his talents working as a councilman since he had been a long-timer of the city. The mayor appointed me to the Community Housing Development Committee because my godfather had recommended me and they needed a minority on the all-white committee. The project director in my opinion was incompetent, but the project continued under his leadership. Keep in mind the city received funds that were allocated to the poorer people and areas to bring their homes up to code. I had a little experience in Oakdale when they asked me to be on a similar committee. As I saw the program then it benefited the realtors not the little guy and decided not to be a part of the Oakdale plan that never got off the ground because too many people saw what I saw. This Modesto plan was a little different, so I thought I would try it for awhile. It is very hard to change things from the outside so you have to try from the inside; therefore, I accepted the challenge. I asked too many questions about the financial affairs of this program and made the chairman quite uncomfortable. The project director fired a black person on his staff, and I tried to get more information on this situation, but because it was a personnel matter I was never fully satisfied.

I felt that the committee should be monitoring the program as directed under the federal guidelines, but I was rebuffed several times. I felt it was a committee that was window dressing for the community, and it was to be a yes committee and approve everything that the director presented. I began to feel I was the Mexican-American token on the committee, and I was suppose to approve everything the staff presented. This wasn't the case, and I recommended to the mayor that the project director be transferred or removed. This did not go over too well, and many of the city fathers thought I was trying to wreck the program. After a few frustrating months, I resigned from the committee. Little did I know that this honest, sincere, inquiring attitude that I had would be the basis of my defeat for Stanislaus County Superintendent election the following June.

My former godfather would take his favorite candidate and introduce him to all the section of the community and had taken him many of the fund raising programs that would have helped me. There were many things that this man did to bring my educational career to a close in Stanislaus county. When the election was over, I came in third out of the race of seven people. I missed the second spot by one hundred and six votes. I guess if I had lost by several hundred, I wouldn't have minded, but this would remain in my mind for many years. This race had a tremendous impact upon me and would influence many of my decisions for years to come. I did meet and get some very fine support from friends that I would cherish the rest of my life. The nine thousand plus votes that I received were a solid honest vote. It was a very strong cross section of people crossing all ethnic, social, and economic groups of people—from the wealthiest businessman in town to the ordinary man on the street. I analyzed my loss for months and months afterward, and I would have to live with that memory the rest of my life. The bottom line for my loss was the lack of money and the psychological pressure on some people to be with a winner. People like a winner and want to associate with one. The money that was spent on advertisement by my opponents was stupendous and outright flagrant for that period and position. The political ethics by some members of their committees was unbelievable during the election. The bias reported by the local newspaper was incomprehensible, and finally, many of those who said they were going to help me did not stand up to the pressure to be counted. There were too many candidates, and each solidified votes for their favorite splitting the vote as following: 10,500, 9,800, 9,700, 4,000, 3,000, 2,000, with 10,000 people not voting and 2,000 votes for a candidate that dropped out early in the race.

The loss of the election had a tremendous impact on me, my family, and my feelings toward the community. It somehow shattered by dreams of being a leader in this community, and it changed the direction of my life for years to come. I had to re-think the value of volunteer organizations because I had put so much time and energy into them. I did not go into these voluntary causes for the express purpose of receiving a reward, but little did I realize that when you speak out on matters you are labeled forever. The individuals who were in charge of some of these organizations were great people, but others were hypocrites when it came to supporting me. Many of these same people did not want to rock the boat and wanted to go along with the crowd. I dropped out of a few organizations immediately because I couldn't stand the hypocrisy displayed by many individuals. I knew regardless of what I did, I would be called a hard loser, but I continued to release my responsibilities with many volunteer organizations. At one time or another I served on many committees and boards such as the Stanislaus Grand Jury, Modesto Housing Commission, Community Concert Association, Region K. Criminal Justice Planning Board, Association of California School Administrators, Association of Community College Administrators, Phi Delta Kappa, University of the Pacific Education Alumni Council, and the Yosemite Area Council. The end of the year I had belonged to one organization, and I was barely working with that one. I found it difficult to have fun and enjoy my family because I had been on the go so much. In American society one has to belong to certain groups, socially and politically, to know the right people, and be at the right place at the right time in order to succeed. It made me very skeptical of what I had been doing for 22 years in education and in my community.

39. Proposition 13

I briefly mentioned Proposition 13 in one of the earlier chapters, but further comments are made here. This proposition which was passed by the electorate in California on June 6, 1978, radically changed the financing of education and public services for years. It caused so many disruptions in people's lives that it would be difficult to list and it had a direct impact upon me and my family. The young Governor was aspiring to be a candidate for the office of U.S. president, and his politically controlled legislature refused to reduce taxes which caused a huge surplus of money to accumulate and they did nothing to alleviate the situation. Little did they know that the initiative process would work as it did. An initiative was placed on the ballot and the electorate overwhelmingly approved it. This required the reduction of property taxes by almost 60%. Public services as well as education depended upon property taxes for their sustenance, but the funds were reduced, which in turn meant services had to be curtailed. The city, county, and all the educational institutions had to cut back immediately. The first cuts at the school levels were made with the school supplies and many of the so-called frills. When the budget had to be tightened more, the various agencies laid off people. This was a tragedy which could have been avoided if the governor and the legislature would have reduced taxes earlier.

Proposition 13 really affected me personally. After twenty-two years in the field of education, I felt that the people of California really didn't care, understand, nor appreciate what the educators have done for the state since at that time the state was at the cutting edge of different programs. Previous governors had been very generous to education and put their budget where their mouths were, but subsequent governors used nothing but platitudes and usually adopted their budgets after the prison and welfare budgets were adopted. This was a message by the people of California to get rid of those ineffective, incompetent, and poorly tenured teachers and administrators. Comments by people on the street were such that educators had it made all this time, now let them see how it is to be insecure and stand in an unemployment line looking for a job. I couldn't believe the editorials that I read regarding the attitude toward teachers. What did we do to cause this wrath of so many? I found it hard to believe—should I stay in the profession? I could understand some of the poorer feelings about education and educators because our profession had individuals in it who should not be teaching. This happens in every profession, but ours is the largest and we are expected to resolve every problem that arises in our society along with teaching students the basics—reading, writing, and arithmetic. I had been a teacher and administrator (up to 1978) at all levels except the university level for twenty-two years and I saw all kinds of teachers and administrators—some good and others poor. I saw a steady decline in the morale of the teaching profession throughout the state; however, there are many reasons, i.e. - low salaries, large classroom sizes, lower standards for students, fewer aspirations from the students. The list is endless!

This initiative affected my attitude toward education, and I almost left it. I had an informal meeting with a personnel officer of one of the largest industries in Modesto. I was not sure but I left the door open in case I decided to make the change—there was a job offer, but I was reluctant to leave education after so many years. I decided to continue looking for another position. I didn't realize that part of my position would be in jeopardy because of this proposition. The superintendent of the district where I was employed decided that he had to tighten his school budget. He got help from a forty-person committee composed of a cross section of the community. This committee was to be used by him to soften his recommendations for further cuts which amounted to a million and a half-dollars. Districts all over the state began cutting back and reducing staff because of the March 1st and 15th deadline set by law. All school employees had to be notified by these dates or else they had to be employed the following year. Some administrators had to make presentations to this advisory body regarding certain programs, and I was chosen to make one for the evening high school program, the one I was responsible for at fifty per-cent of my salary. The other part of my salary was paid for by another district. I prepared a fifteen-minute presentation for the advisory committee, and they gave me some fine commendations regarding how efficient and effective I was with the number of dollars that were allocated for the program.

The committee heard over sixty-five hours of presentations regarding the district's finances and would have been very useful if the superintendent had used their recommendations but unfortunately he didn't. The committee strongly recommended that the evening high school program remain intact because it provided a very useful function and alternative for the students to receive their high school diplomas. I was asked by the assistant superintendent of business to present the same report to the board of education at 10 p.m. one evening so they could have additional information regarding my program. They received my presentation with very few questions; however, the former president of the school board went out of her way to strongly praise the program. She indicated how unique it was in the state and she would brag about the program everywhere she went. I felt fairly good about my presentation, and I felt there was no need to worry about my program or job being curtailed. Little did I know that the superintendent still harbored a deep resentment toward me for not supporting his candidate for the County Schools position—his candidate lost during the run off, and I supported the individual that won. His candidate spent over $24,000.00 in the campaign expenses for the county superintendent position (much of it his own money) and lost the election by a wide margin. I felt my support for the other candidate had a lot to do with it, and I knew many people in the educational community would be very angry with me. The superintendent decided at the last moment to make the recommendation that the evening high school program be consolidated with the vocational program and that I be reassigned to the classroom. The district vocational director would take over the responsibilities of the evening high school position. He would later resign and work as a financial manager because he could not approve of the behavior that was going on in the district office.

I discovered this recommendation on the morning of February twelfth when a so-called friend awoke me out of a dead sleep on a Sunday morning and asked me if I read the morning papers. The newspaper stated I was to be reassigned to the classroom. That was the first I had heard and knew of the superintendent's move to get back at me for not being loyal to him. I didn't know what to do at first, but I kept cool and calm as possible while I read the morning paper. How could a man do this to someone else without at least informing him? This man had quite a reputation for being a tough administrator, but when it hit me I thought differently. My wife and I went to three public hearings where the board listened to the various proposals, but not once did anyone come to my support or support the program that I was administering—not even the so-called friend who woke me up that early Sunday morning.

Finally, after two days of hearings, I sat down and composed a two-page statement regarding the program and how it was administered. There were five basic questions which I asked, and I answered them. I thought long and hard before I made the decision to deliver the letters personally to each board member. Was this the thing to do? Was this the professional method to handle this difficult situation? Was this the ethical process to do directly to the board members and by-pass the superintendent and the management team? All the answers to these questions were in the affirmative. The board members only hear the superintendent's point of view, and he tells them what they want to hear. This particular board rarely ever disagreed with the superintendent. How can a board go against a person whom they have appointed and hired—someone would lose face? Therefore, I felt direct contact with the board member would be our approach. No one in the management team or the teachers association called me or asked if I needed help. These organizations had inept and weak leadership; therefore, they could not stand up to the superintendent if they wanted to. I disregarded those organizations and decided not to waste my time asking for their help. By the time they would get around to it, the whole affair would be over. The advisory committee was in strong support of my program and mentioned to me that I had made the best presentation of all the administrators. Several members of the committee called the board of trustees but no commitment was made on their part. Later members of the advisory committee found out by way of the media all their work was in vain. They were criticized by the chairman of the board, and he informed them they were an advisory committee and their recommendations did not have any influence over the final decision. The board had asked the superintendent to compile a list of recommendations, and the board had too abided by his recommendations. In essence, the advisory committee was window dressing for the community. Too often committees are used this way, and many hours of time are just wasted and good people are turned off by this process and never again help with the community activities. My wife and I delivered the statements to each board member and waited for a reply—none came. We went to the next to last hearing before the final decisions were to be made about my reassignment. The various organizations made oral comments on all aspects of the superintendent's recommendations to no avail. The advisory committee which I thought would be my strongest supporters didn't say a word about my program nor did any others at the meeting. I was at a total loss for words. No one would rally to my support. After the assistant superintendent of curriculum delivered a blistering attack toward the teaching association's leadership, I felt I had to speak directly to the board in an executive session because it was not my nature to criticize the agency with whom I worked publicly. When the board broke for a ten-minute recess, I asked the chairman if I could meet with the board in executive session. He said, yes, and about eight o'clock that evening I met with the superintendent's executive council and the board of education.

This was the first time in my twenty-two years in the profession, that this ever happened to me. You can't imagine how alone I was with unfriendly people at my back and the very stoic board members in front of me. I was well prepared with statistics that made the assistant superintendent of business look a little inept. That was not my intention, but the poor man was just not competent for the position. By the way, this wasn't his first time he was in this situation because his computations would change every time there was a different meeting. The poor fellow had to resign from a position in a mid-west city because he couldn't handle the job—how long would be remain here? He could not correct or refute any of my figures or data when I asked him too in front of the board. The superintendent said in the open session before the executive session that the reason for this recommendation was because of belt tightening, and it was unfortunate we had to do this; therefore, we shouldn't talk about this in open session because of personalities involved. He immediately cut off the discussion in the open session when a board member asked for the recommendations and said we will discuss this in executive session. Little did he know that I would be alone in the room to defend the program and inform the board how this recommendation arrived at this idea. I asked a few questions in order to get a few preliminaries out of the way and then permitted the superintendent to defend his recommendation to consolidate my program and to send me back to the classroom. I presented information that the board was not aware of, and I certainly got their attention. The superintendent had a way of showing his nervousness—he would put his hand to support his chin and then would stroke his upper lip quickly. This went on almost throughout my presentation. I stopped after about twenty minutes and asked the chairman if anyone in the room had any question or corrections regarding my presentation. I said please correct me or refute anything I said in this session. No one did; therefore, everything I said including my closing statement was true. It went like this, "This recommendation by the superintendent is purely a personal vindictive vendetta against an administrator who does his job professionally but who acts independently in matters which do not concern his employment responsibilities." There was no response to that comment, so I thanked the board and excused myself. Later, I found out there was no further discussion of this matter in executive session. The next evening the board made the decision which would affect my life and many lives in the community.

Yes, Proposition 13 really was going to hit our district as well as every school district in the state of California. At last, the common person could speak out and tell the public agencies in our state what they wanted. This was the march toward the decline of the once proud and high-ranking California's educational system. Funding for education would be at the mercy of the politicians in Sacramento and normally be approved after the prison and welfare budgets. Soon, the state which ranked fourth in the nation for funding schools would rank forty-fourth—a prediction I made when I campaigned for County Superintendent of schools (1978). Did they really want this to happen to their educational system? It is safe to say that many educators voted for this initiative because they were disgusted with the governmental system in our state. Many teachers felt this would never pass because it was tried in the past, and it always failed. The only difference this time was that we had a multimillion-dollar surplus in Sacramento and a governor and legislature that gave no sign of giving relief to the public. After it passed, the people felt nothing would change because someone would help the districts that needed help. Well, the public found out differently. You can't have your cake and eat it too. Services had to be reduced and that is what this board had to do-lay off people who provided services in order to save money. They started with the elementary school budget and then proceeded to the high school budget. When they got to my position and program, the chairman changed the wording which should have read, "the reduction of the evening high school program and a reassignment of the evening high school principal to the classroom." Everyone in the audience knew why this was being done, but no one made a comment. As soon as the chairman finished making the changes, one of the newer board members said, "I want no part of this recommendation and this program should remain as it is." He said, "I vote that we drop this item from any further discussion." The next board member said, "I agree." The next two who helped appoint the superintendent said, "The district is getting more than its money's worth from the principal and he is doing an excellent job. We recommend that to leave it as it is." The chairman and the next board member said, "I agree with those statements—it is a well operated program." The last board member (who was a dentist) said, "I think his salary is out of proportion to the budget." He didn't know the assistant superintendent of business had asked me only to present the expenses and not the total income. The budget would have been twice as large and the salary would have been in the right proportion if I done that. A futile attempt by the superintendent was made for further discussion, and he indicated many more dollars would be saved by his recommendation. The chairman looked at him with disgust and asked if there were any more questions on this item. There were none, and it was voted six to one to drop this item from the superintendent's recommendation. Several people in the audience turned around and looked and me and my wife with a smile. This item was difficult to find in the newspaper.

I was very relieved of the outcome, but I knew that I had to look for another job immediately. I could not work with a person who was so vindictive. All during the week, board members, associates, members of my immediate staff called or dropped by the office congratulating me for the action of the board. They were really telling me that I had the guts to stand up against all odds and face someone that they couldn't. I pondered the "congratulations" for weeks after the decision was made to keep me on as a principal of the Evening High School. I won the battle but did I win the war? This man would try and use all kinds of tactics to harass me so I would lose my cool. I really couldn't believe that this was happening to me after all of these dedicated years in the teaching profession. The democratic way of life—it is whom you know not what you know that counts in this country. I won four times over this superintendent's recommendation. The first was when I was appointed to the principalship over his favorite candidate; second, I strongly supported the elective process for the county superintendent's position; third, I supported another candidate and the superintendent's candidate lost; and, fourth, I influenced the board to a six to one decision to drop his recommendation to eliminate the evening high school principal's position. He would not forget and his influence in the educational community hurt my chances for further advancement when it came time for me to move. I had to take the initiative and make the next move. It would be very uncomfortable working with his lackeys and I wanted out of this district. His clique did basically what he wanted them to do—you don't rock the boat, and you'll get ahead in the educational community.

At last I felt free in spirit—I told the board a little of what this man was like and they listened. There was some justice when they listened and voted in my favor. I also knew that my days at this level of education were numbered because this superintendent,— even though he was disliked by many—had much influence with the state administrative association, and he would prevent me from getting any other position in the state. Isn't it strange that educators are like sheep because most administrators keep their mouths shut in public—lest they invoke the wrath of their bosses. Too few practicing administrators write articles honestly describing the ludicrous conditions they face each day. The higher you go in the social and economic strata of education, the more your principles are compromised in order to "get ahead." This is very true in the field of education and one dares not criticize too loudly or you'll find yourself without friends or any means of livelihood. My fight was a lonely one although some of my colleagues provided consolation and sympathy; they never could go beyond giving advice.

40. Rough Around the Edges

I began looking for another position but it was difficult. I did not know the right people and the job market was very bleak. The President of Columbia College retired and I applied for the position to no avail. It was obvious from the start that the superintendent and a board member from that area wanted someone from out of the district, but I applied for the position knowing this. The usual job announcements, letters, and charade were preformed in order to make absolutely sure that the affirmative action rules were abided by. I was interviewed by the superintendent, personnel director, dean of instruction, custodian, student and two staff members. This was a rather strange group, but the superintendent was on the committee to make sure they picked the right person. In 1979 that meant a WASP from the Columbia area. The director of personnel was there in order to make it look legitimate as far as affirmative action was concerned. He was Hispanic and I didn't expect much from him. Before going into the interview, I met the retiring president and he asked me what I was doing there? I said I was being interviewed for the presidency—he said tough luck and smiled. I knew exactly what that meant! I didn't have a chance, and he was right. I left the interview a little sick but confident that I had done my best with the interview. After talking to another candidate, I knew my chances were nil. The superintendent picked four people for the board to interview, but he had already known which one the board members would accept. In order to follow the guideline, he picked a woman, another minority (an Indian), a dean who was second in command, and the man he knew the board would accept. (The latter he went to graduate school with.) He was an ordinary WASP with very little community involvement but he had the credentials that would make him very acceptable to the superintendent, the community, and the board. The board had hired all the top central office officials from outside the district, and they wanted to continue the trend with this appointment. No one in the district had a chance for the position and we all knew it. One thing unusual happened this time. The superintendent visited me after the interview and told me that I had outstanding papers and everything was in good order, but my interviewing techniques and approach to the committee needed some help. He told me that I came on a little strong (a little rough around the edges) and that the committee was a little uneasy with me. He spent a half-hour with me and I guess I was supposed to feel grateful for this visit and his advice.

I guess, looking back over the years, I did express myself too forcefully at the meeting. But how does one display your varied experiences to a committee that usually has its mind pretty well made up? I am sure they felt threatened because I knew too much about the school, community, and the staff. After the superintendent's visit to my office, I knew fully well that my days at this institution were numbered if I wanted to advance professionally. I had to look at myself and my profession very seriously within the next few years— could I survive? I applied for the dean of instruction position that opened up in the district only to inform the boys at the top that I was interested. When the job description was released it was designed for someone on the staff. A specific sentence stating that a vocational background was needed, I knew that I didn't have a chance. I had an academic background, so that gave the personnel director the opportunity to eliminate my name from the list of qualified persons. I think I had a good case for a change of discrimination but I was in a very tenuous position. If I screamed foul and sued the district, I would have been black-balled forever from any community college district. I needed these hypocrites in order to obtain a position where I could have some authority. Another problem loomed over my head—Proposition 9 (1980), which was going to cut state income taxes by fifty percent, was going to be voted upon on June 3, 1980. If passed this would further erode the financial support for community colleges.

I was about to have an interview for the dean of instruction position in southern California and it looked very promising because the Chancellor was Hispanic, and he was interested in my background. The morning of the interview the personnel director of that district called and said the interview was being canceled because the district was freezing all hirings because of the budget crunch. This was the beginning of doors closing for me at other districts. I guess my journey in the educational field was that I was not at the right place at the right time nor did I start developing my network early enough in my career.

41. An Affirmative Action Perspective

My experiences with other Mexican-American educators has been an interesting and curious one. My experience regarding affirmative action arose when I dealt with Mexican-American educators – would they have that position if there had been no affirmative action? In my opinion, a good minority would have never gotten into the front door of an institution if affirmative action wasn't available. At one institution a teacher from a Southwestern state, who was only a 6th grade school teacher with no college experience, was hired as a counselor at a college because that college had to have a token Hispanic on their staff. Later they hired a few more in other disciplines – out of a total of two hundred and fifty staff members there were only seven Spanish surnames on the staff. Now that the push for women teachers/administrators is taking place, many Boards/Trustees are hiring "white females" and are by-passing the minorities completely. Several institutions in the San Joaquin Valley have their token Mexican-American administrator, but the California Junior College system had (in 1978) very few Mexican-American Presidents out of one hundred and six community colleges.

I feel that it doesn't make a difference to the hiring practices if there is a Hispanic President. My experience has been they would rather hire a "white" than a "brown" in order to save face with the individuals with whom they associate. An example: I had an interview with a President of Mexican descent at a Southwestern city. I pass the initial screening committee and I was one of three to be interviewed by the President. I arrived about two hours early, but the President was too busy to meet with me. The secretary was very nice and showed me the way to a fine restaurant. I had lunch and then met with the President. As I sized him up, he did the same with me. The questions that he asked were so inadequate, I felt embarrassed at the lack of knowledge this man had. I really began to wonder, how did this man get his job. Well, I found out how a little later after his futile attempt with my interview. He drove me to the site where a new campus was going to be built and we talked philosophy along the way. I said to myself—this would be a fantastic opportunity to be the Dean of Instruction at this school. We drove around the site and city for an hour or so and then we went back to the central office. During this time he told me how he got the job as President. He said, "It is whom you know, that's how." He started his career as a junior high teacher in the southwest and then became a junior high principal. He was working on this doctorate and during his research and he read about the opening in the Chronicle of Higher Education. A need for an Assistant to the Vice Chancellor of Student Services at a large university. This was the era of strong affirmative action and student unrest. He applied and was hired as a token by the university system. He told me he took plenty of "heat from the students" and it really bothered to him. He also, said "that if it wasn't for affirmative action, he wouldn't have made it there." Well, he kept his contacts in the Southwest and his friend told him this presidency would be available if he wanted it. With the title and experience at a university system, it was a cinch for him to get that job. The only problem as far as I could see, he knew nothing about the community college system. As his supervisor said—"You can learn it and surround yourself with competent staff and bluff it until you become the expert." Well, I was in a different position and I observed that he didn't know anything about the community college system, and I did. Later, when we had a beer at the airport, I knew I didn't get the job. He didn't want the competition and he wanted an anglo. I later found out that his staff had a small ratio of Mexican-American teachers compared to the anglos. I found it difficult to accept the fact that many Mexicans in high position in education and other professions do not look back to help other aspiring Mexicans. They are either insecure in their roles and do not wish to have any competition or they may think—"Well, I had to work my head off to get where I am, let them do it also." I have even found that some Hispanics in the profession will badmouth other Mexicans at committee meetings and even vote to keep them from getting a higher positions.

When a controversial issue arises in a discussion, they will not defend or support another Mexican. I know that my background is much different than the average Mexican who was born in the barrios or in an area where there was a preponderance of Mexicans. I was born and reared in a very small community where I was sometimes the only Mexican in the classroom all through elementary school. I really never saw a group of the same color until the weekends when we played football or basketball in our neighborhood. I never really had a close Mexican-American friend while I was going to elementary school. This has had a tremendous bearing on my attitude toward affirmative action.

42. The Last Lap

My search for advancement and professional growth was a very frustrating and difficult part of my career. It was difficult for a person who did not have a "network" set up and/or contacts at the community college level of education. Another thing that made it difficult was my unbending stubbornness against appeasing anyone or "brown-nosing." I wasn't a glad-hander or a politician, because I thought that supervisors would reward professional growth and excellence. Seeing and hearing all the good work that one had done would help for advancement and promotion. It was very hard for me to accept the idea that it was "whom you know" and "not what you know" that gave people promotions.

During the late '60s and early '70s affirmative action was in full bloom. Many institutions grabbed any minority if he/she could just breathe. They really didn't care how qualified they were. This resulted in many very poorly trained and many incompetents being hired. This worked well for many top white administrators, because they could then say, "I told you so," when that minority failed. I never really wanted to be in that "bag," so I continued to work hard and grow educationally. In many respects I think I became over-qualified and some on interviewing committees resented that.

I applied for Vice President of Instruction at a southern California community college. I think that had to be one of the worst situations that I have ever experienced. The president was rude, curt, and outright disrespectful. The committee was composed of all men who were just as rude. I was glad I was not offered that job although the president called later to apologize and told me why I wasn't hired. Later, I found out they hired an Asian woman. This helped them with their minority and female statistics. I then tried at a Central Valley community college knowing full well that the conservatives in that area would be difficult to overcome. I was selected for two interviews. The first was a very pleasant, sincere and honest interview. The committee consisted of five staff members, plus a student and the superintendent. I passed the interview (the first ever) and my name was submitted to the board. I felt very confident, but the conservative views in the area bothered me. The second interview was disappointing. The superintendent did all the talking and rehashed some of the same questions I had during the first one. I felt I did much better at the first one and this was apparent when they chose a white woman who had a Spanish surname. Again, I had more educational background than she (MA or Ed.D.) but I didn't have the practical experience that she had whatever that was. This is a device used by many screening committees and superintendents to select the individuals they want and use the law in their favor. Again, affirmative action was being adhered to in order to help their statistics. I felt very bad about all the tricks of the trade that were used to prevent me or other Mexican-Americans from obtaining top leadership positions at the community college level.

I did not let these poor experiences stop me form applying at different colleges. After sending many resumes, I received my chance at interviews. A very honest college was along the coast for a vice president position. The paper-screening device was very difficult. Many items had to be prepared before completing the necessary requirements. I did complete them and was asked for an interview. The president did say they were looking for a minority, but I didn't take him seriously. He was really a glad hander and later I found out he was high on the list of names in one of the largest and strongest associations in California. The president met me on schedule, but several committee members were late. We got started a little late but ended on time. It was a very sterile interview because the questions were read without any emotion to them. I tried to answer them to the best of by ability but somehow did not come across very well. The president had the courtesy of calling me and indicated to me that my name would not be submitted to the board as one of the final three. That was the first and only time that kind of explanation was done in any of my interviews. Usually, you receive a very cold letter saying someone else got the job and thanking you for applying. What else can you expect? Well, he was sincere in his hiring a Mexican -American all right but he hired him because he knew him very well. They had served on several accreditation teams together and worked on their doctoral programs at a leading university together. They also had their Ph.D. in a science. This told me something else about the hiring practices at this level of education—you must use a network!

I had the good fortune of serving on a screening committee for the selection of a president. I think I was placed on this committee because I was a minority and the superintendent wanted to make me feel good because of certain things that happened to me with two vacancies that occurred in the district. I received an interview, but never came close to the finals. He later told me that I was too aggressive and "rough around the edges." This is what the superintendent told a board member who was a close friend of mine. Apparently I gave the impression to the committee that I knew too much. I was trying to impress the superintendent with how much I did know but I guess I over did it because the committee must have objected. Being on this presidential committee helped me grow a little. I saw how other committee members were promoted to higher positions, because they used that initial contact with the new person as an entree when he came aboard. I thought of that as I helped interview the candidate. It was a very pleasant experience and the superintendent tried very hard to give the impression that he was going to use the committee's decision. The paper screening went very smooth and the committee narrowed it down to twelve and then to six. Then after many debates it was narrowed to four and all local candidates were eliminated. This was pretty well engineered and I felt sorry for the two local candidates who could have done the job, but were eliminated because they didn't have the experience or the degrees. The district always made a big show of sending some members to the area where the potential person worked. Naturally they heard the thing they wanted to hear. Well, they selected an individual that was not my top choice. He did have many experiences, but only at one college. The candidate that I wanted declined and was hired at another district.

Well, my experience with the "new" president was an interesting one. He really did nothing for several months and the two deans did most of the work around the school. He was from out of state so he had to learn all over again. He spent more time behind closed doors than any person I've known. Well, after several months went by he issued his reorganization plan. This plan caused more aggravation with the staff than any other thing that he did. He listened very closely to the faculty leadership. Well, he moved many people around including me, but lied to me in the process. I've never forgiven him for that. He told several other people what he planned to do with me under the pretence that it was an upward move and that I needed other experiences. When I asked him about my future he told me, but he said he had only spoken to the two deans. I found out he talked to many before he had ever talked to me. When asked about a deanship here, he said he didn't know. When I asked why, he fudged and then finally said some member of the staff didn't like the way I came into the college system. Mainly one counselor who never had to work in his life and became a counselor right out of college. There were others like this giving him advice about administrators. People, who were new to the college system, but gained leadership roles in the faculty senate told him I was a little "cold" and "aloof." I asked him if I had a chance at any future positions and he said "not at this college." This was really a blow to my work ethic. All the things that I had done effectively and efficiently were for naught. How would I grow professional anywhere, if I would not make it in my home territory.

This president only lasted three years. Most presidents start looking for a new position as soon as they arrive at the new one. He was no different and he left after three year. The superintendent took over the role as president and things settled down. Not much was done at the college level because we were in a down mode—low enrolment and income. Regardless, he was financially rewarded by the board for this period.

Then the district promoted one of the area deans to instruction and later to president. A lot of shifting and jockeying around with different responsibilities were being done with the "in" group. For some reason I was never in that group. Not much change took place during his tenure even though the leaders of the faculty demanded it. A couple of administrative positions were eliminated to free up money for salary increases. These were hard times at the community college level.

The superintendent/chancellor retired and his successor was chosen. She had worked her way up as a part-time instructor, tenured instructor, director and assistant chancellor. She had done all the right things, but did not have any administration leadership positions at the college level. After an extensive nation-wide search she was selected. Affirmative action for women was in full bloom at this district because several central office positions previously held by men were now being filled by women. When the president retired, a Hispanic woman with very little experience was selected against the strong opposition of faculty. When the Vice President of Instruction left for another school and his position was filled after a nation-wide search by a person with virtually no experience, I felt it was time for me to leave and I retired after forty-two years in the profession.

Affirmative action was repealed by the people in California in 1996 and even though it was used against me in my quest for a higher position, I think it is a step backward. There is still much racism in academia and the general public.

43. The Final Straw

After forty-two years (two years of accumulative sick leave) teaching and having been an administrator as all levels from K-6 to the junior college I decided to retire. My education experiences had been varied enough to keep me interested and interesting for my students and peers. I have been asking myself what has changed during the past four decades and I say "not so much." The State of California, once the flagship and leader in education, now ranks almost at the bottom next to the State of Mississippi. The budget for education is determined after the welfare and prison budgets are adopted. Prison guards make more money than the average school teacher, and teachers are shown little respect by parents and public officials. Schools are asked to solve all the social problems because dysfunctional families are unable to. Every two/four years we hear our politicians say how important education is, but they rarely live up to their words.

The years passed but not without problems for me in academia. Since starting in February of 1956 as a substitute teacher at a high school to the final years as a faculty member of junior college, I always found it difficult getting a promotion or an advancement. I've often wondered if it were my personality or resentment and jealousy of those around me. As one superintendent at the college level told me, "You were a little rough around the edges," whatever that meant. I was straight forward and was honest and sincere to everyone, and this sometimes made individuals uncomfortable because I didn't tell them what they wanted to hear. When I applied and obtained a junior high vice principal position, the principal resigned because he would not work with a Mexican-American. When I applied and obtained a K-6 principalship, the woman chairperson told me I didn't have the experiences for the job. Thank goodness she was overruled, or I would never have been given the experience. When I applied and received the Evening High School/Assistant Dean of Continuing Education position at the Junior College, it was against the desire of the Assistant Superintendent and Superintendent of City Schools because the superintendent had promised one of his buddies the position. Again, they were overruled! An earlier chapter discusses the problems I had with that superintendent for not joining his team.

I had to go through a second interview of junior college administrators before I was appointed. When I was promoted to an Assistant Dean of Instruction the vocal leaders of the faculty were in an uproar because they were not consulted. Three staff members complained that I had never taught at the college - yet I taught ten years as a part-time instructor; five years English As A Second Language; and five years conversational Spanish. These were not credit classes, therefore, they didn't count according to the vocal faculty leaders. I have found that if there is a "good teacher" with knowledge and experience you could teach at any level. I applied for various positions at the college. I was always told I didn't have the experience. Finally, when I applied for the Vice President of Student Services I was told by two members of the screening committee that I was the "wrong color" and "sex." An African-American women got the position, and she had very little experience. Since then, the district has hired several African American women, as well as individuals with Hispanic sounding names, to high level positions in order to bring their statistics up as desired by the Chancellor.

This leads me into the subject of affirmative action and state proposition 209 (1996). I never took advantage of the affirmative action program because I felt it was designed basically for African-Americans. Many of them would never have gotten into high level positions if it were not for this policy. All we have to do is look at the Supreme Court to see one African American who used the system to the fullest. When the President appointed him, he said, "he was the most qualified judge in the United States." The President must have choked on those words because we all know differently. Since then, the judge has made some very startling decisions that usually followed one of the more conservative justices on the Supreme Court. That justice after being put through the "hanging by the television," made the comment he would be making many decisions for a long time that would effect his own race as well as others. Yet, we have other African American leaders who are for affirmative action and know deep in their hearts they would not have risen to their respective positions without it.

I left the educational profession feeling good for what I had accomplished, but with mixed emotions that maybe I could have helped others a little more. The present social and political climate requires that all of those minorities and women who have struggled beyond the barriers of social, educational and political injustices must look back and help those who are trying to advance. The idea that "I made it by my boot straps" is fine, but, really, no one can honestly say "they" made it by themselves. Just think of these teachers, professors, deans or presidents of a college who have said something to help you with a little more direction and assurance that you too can be there someday.

Someone told me that when you see things in education being advocated now that you did not twenty-five years ago, it is time to retire. Examples as teaching reading by phonics, returning to immersion in the English language (which didn't work) and returning to basic math. All of these proposals were tried years ago, but those who want to impress the boards and public now put a different twist to the terminology. For instance, we always had two, three yearly planning schedules. Today they call that "blue skying" or some type "Vision 2000." We always had good discussions over different issues. Now we call that "collaboration."

My father and mother would have been very proud of my personal accomplishments. Most parents wanted the best for their children and tried very hard to give them all the opportunities possible so as to succeed. My parents were very limited financially to help me or my brothers and sisters, but they remained married together for all of their lives. That gave us all a good foundation for our personal lives.

I guess in retrospect I can still see the eyes of that cowboy on his horse staring down at me and my mother while his horse and cattle destroyed her flower garden. If it hadn't been for that incident

Julius C. Manrique, Ed.D.

I may not have struggled so hard for my education and endured the pain and frustration that I encountered on my journey through life.

I close in hoping anyone who reads this material will use some of my experiences to better themselves socially, economically, educationally and politically.

www.ingramcontent.com/pod-product-compliance
Lightning Source LLC
Chambersburg PA
CBHW030320290526
45785CB00001B/450

* 9 7 8 0 7 5 9 6 3 8 0 8 2 *